THE INESCAPABLE CALLING

THE INESCAPABLE CALLING

*The missionary task of the church of Christ
in the light of contemporary challenge
and opportunity*

by

R. KENNETH STRACHAN

WILLIAM B. EERDMANS PUBLISHING COMPANY
GRAND RAPIDS, MICHIGAN

To

GRACE STRACHAN ROBERTS

Kenneth Strachan's sister,
who with practical, loving deeds
daily answers God's inescapable calling

ELIZABETH STRACHAN
(MRS. R. KENNETH)

EDITORIAL FOREWORD

Christian World Mission Books are intended to provide teachers and students of missions and church history, pastors and concerned laymen, and the general public with the full range of books needed to fill the gaps in the literature on the world mission of the church of Christ. They include history, current survey, studies in missionary theory and practice, functional emphases and methods, special topics of importance, biography, and source material not easily available. Authors are drawn from many nations and denominations. Protestants — Evangelical and Ecumenical, Roman Catholics, and hopefully Orthodox are included. All are men and women of sound scholarship and of experience and authority in their respective fields. The books will contribute to knowledge and, it is hoped, to dialogue on the meaning and effective means of mission in the creative new era now opening.

The present book is part of the series, "Ministries in Missions." The books in this series treat the various functional emphases within the mission. Basic to all activities, and in light of which they must all be judged, is evangelism. The first book in the series is this posthumous work of the late R. Kenneth Strachan, general director of the Latin America Mission and one of the foremost missionary statesmen of the present time.

R. PIERCE BEAVER
Editor

CONTENTS

9

PREFACE

When Dr. Kenneth Strachan died in February, 1965, some of us who had worked closely with him found ourselves benumbed by our loss and bewildered by the strange ways of God. Here was a beloved friend and a choice servant of God, seemingly snatched away from us at the very height of his powers. We were mystified, and we found solace in silence.

After the period of mute shock had passed, a few of us were discussing our cherished memories of him. Again and again reference was made to one basic element that seemed most accurately to describe his life and ministry. With almost monotonous consistency, each of us spoke of Ken's utter transparency, his sheer, unshadowed honesty in dealing with himself and with others.

At that time none of us had yet seen the manuscript of *The Inescapable Calling*. If we had, we might have stopped groping for words, glad to adopt a phrase that he himself had used. For in dealing with the elements that qualify Christians for effective witness, he had written that, next to our own personal experience of the grace of God, the most important factor is "the constant recollection of our own humanity."

Whatever else Ken Strachan was, he was a man of God

11

who was characterized by the constant recollection of his own humanity. This was the way we knew him: a friend and colleague who wore no mask and who seemed forever aware that he was a frail child of the dust, and feeble as frail. No false modesty was involved, and if we sometimes felt that he too often downgraded himself and his work, there was never any question that it was his understanding of God's greatness that kept him, moment by moment, conscious of his own frailty and inadequacy. And he was able to demand honesty of others because he had first been ruthlessly honest with himself.

The lectures he gave at Fuller Theological Seminary during the last year of his life, here presented in edited form, are based on an insistence that, in times like these, we all need to be characterized by "the constant recognition of our own humanity." Dr. Strachan's voice is not heard in the strident chorus of critics proclaiming the death of God, or the irrelevance of the church, or the ineffectiveness of the missionary enterprise. But he has faced squarely the tragic slowness of many in the church to understand its mission, and honesty has compelled him to point out the frailty of many of our ecclesiastical institutions. We have not understood our Lord, and we have not understood our vocation. Our efforts to serve the Lord have been marked more by the evidences of our human limitations than by the presence of his all-sufficient power — and Dr. Strachan insists that we plead guilty to some of the charges that have been made against us.

Yet the voice of honesty need not be a cry of despair, nor a mere sad wailing over our failures. In the Word of God and in the history of the early church, the author finds abundant grounds for hope. The same honesty that leads him to expose our fallible humanity makes him quick to remind us of victories that can yet be won, through a Power not our own.

God purposes the evangelization of his world, and he raises up men like Kenneth Strachan, who see more clearly than the rest of us how a sovereign Lord works through redeemed humanity to bring his purposes to pass. The basic presuppositions of Evangelism-in-Depth are not abstract theories; they are descriptions of the ways in which God has been observed to work. When Dr. Strachan wrote *The Inescapable Calling*, these basic elements had already been tested in real-life situations. Since his death, their validity has been even more fully confirmed in the experience of country after country in Latin America.

Beginning in Nicaragua in 1960, a series of Evangelism-in-Depth efforts has provided the proving grounds where the principles enunciated in this book were tested. The evangelical church, a tiny minority in these countries, faced up to the scriptural insistence that an abundant reaping depends on abundant sowing. Believers were mobilized for witness as never before, and new forms and media of witness were utilized and coordinated for the effective spread of the gospel. Costa Rica (1961) and Guatemala (1962) became the scenes of something that approached total mobilization, and these countries were evangelized as they never had been before.

Moreover, Strachan's insistence that Christians can and must work together (solidly based on the scriptural teaching that Christian unity must be both visible and functional) was carried into practice in these lands and in Honduras (1964) and Venezuela (1964). Christians of many different denominational and undenominational groups saw this subject of Christian unity in a new light: not only was such unity a pragmatic necessity if the evangelistic task was to be accomplished; it was, above all else, the will of God for his church.

And what of Dr. Strachan's reminder to the church that when Christians pool their resources, God multiplies them? The nations already mentioned have an answer for that question, and so do the people of God in Bolivia and in the Dominican Republic, where Evangelism-in-Depth was the program of the church in 1965 and 1966. Pressed for finances and for personnel, harassed by revolution and bloodshed, these believers offered up to God what they had — and saw a twentieth-century repetition of the multiplication of the loaves and the fishes.

A fourth presupposition of Evangelism-in-Depth, that a dedicated minority can make an impact on an entire nation, is incredible by any human standard. It would seem like the wistful hope of an armchair strategist, a beautiful ideal, impossible of realization, if we had not seen just this happen in country after country. As I write these words, the truth of this amazing claim is being demonstrated once again — this time in Peru, where a tiny fraction of the total population is challenging the entire nation with the claims of Christ.

So Dr. Strachan's theses, so clearly enunciated in *The Inescapable Calling*, are being battle-tested today. And from the results of this testing, Christians all over the world are taking fresh courage and are moving out in new efforts to make the Savior known to their nations. Aware of their own humanity, but strengthened by the presence and power of God, they are gladly engaging in "the inescapable calling," and rejoicing as they see God moving mightily in our day.

Lutterworth Press has kindly given permission to quote a number of passages from *Upon the Earth*, by Daniel T. Niles. Grateful acknowledgment is also due to Miss Susan Roberts, Dr. Strachan's niece, and Miss Clara Strachan, his daughter, for preparation of the indexes found at the end of this book.

HORACE L. FENTON, JR.

CONTEMPORARY CHALLENGE
TO MISSION

I

THE INESCAPABLE CALLING

"Necessity is laid upon me. Woe to me if I do not preach the gospel!"

MOST CHRISTIANS HAVE A GUILTY CONSCIENCE ABOUT WITNESSING. Actually they do very little of it; but they can never let the subject alone. Hence, the innumerable sermons and exhortations, the torrent of books and articles, the endless conferences and the continuous study and discussion of the subject. One of the curious inner tensions of the Christian life is this conflict between the obligation to share the gospel and the general disinclination to do so. Whether the Christian wills it or not, necessity is laid upon him; he cannot get rid of the sense of responsibility.

Today the subject of witness and evangelism is more pressing than ever. There are various reasons for this.

First, Christianity as a world faith, and the Christian church as the embodiment and institutionalization of that faith, are actually engaged in a desperate struggle for survival. In spite of the great material prosperity of Christian

17

churches in some parts of the world, and notwithstanding the encouraging emergence of young dynamic churches in others, questions regarding the validity and credibility of Christianity's traditional affirmations and institutions are rising to haunt many a churchman. Much of the Christian tradition seems irrelevant to the citizens of the world.

Yet there is evidence that along with the growing indifference in some quarters, there is an openness to the Christian message almost unique in history. This is true not only among the so-called Christian nations of the West, but also to some extent among the non-Christian nations of the East. This openness may be due to the world's growing maturity in matters of religious freedom and tolerance. Likewise it may stem from an unconscious sense of need. But the fact is that today men of all stations are open to the gospel (though not necessarily willing to accept it) as never before.

The king trembled when he saw Daniel in the lions' den, and modern rulers, like Darius of old, are also wondering if Christianity holds the answers. Confronted with man's helplessness before the economic and political lions of his own creation, they are in effect calling out in pagan anguish, "Christian, has your god whom you serve been able to deliver you?" (Dan. 6:20). Or to change the figure, human society, like the mariners of Jonah's day, is caught up in the raging storms that assault modern civilization and is absorbed in a desperate struggle for survival. It too is turning in effect to the Christian with the cry, "Arise, and call upon your God . . . that we do not perish" (Jonah 1:6).

Still another reason for giving attention to the responsibility of the Christian in witness is to be found in the current demand for updating Christian methods of evangelism. The urgency of this task is highlighted by the development of new media and techniques which, in turn, are based on deeper insights into human behavior, both in the individual and in the community. Certainly it is beyond dispute that in this modern world of exploding population, rapid social change, economic stress and revolution, the church of Jesus Christ faces new challenges and opportunities.

But there is a still more significant reason for the current interest in evangelism. It is the unmistakable evidence of the working of the Holy Spirit in the midst of his people and in the midst of the current world revolution that is causing Christians to lift up their eyes to ponder their God-given mission. More compelling than the secular world's threat to the continued existence of Christianity, or the opportunity presented by the current situation, or the challenge of new media and techniques of communication, is the sense of a divine moving in the events of today, reminding us of the prophetic promises of final victory and judgment. All of these factors are undoubtedly back of the present widespread effort to rediscover the mission of the church and to recover its dynamic.

Already this study and reappraisal, carried out in many quarters under varied auspices, has resulted in an abundant literature[1] on almost every aspect of mission and evangelism. Fresh insights into biblical truth as it relates to modern conditions promise to define the mission of the church in new terms. These insights may also make necessary the reform of existing structures, and the introduction of new patterns of church life and witness, involving the church and its members in a new relationship to the world.

A fresh wind is blowing. Whether in the fullest sense it is biblically inspired remains to be seen. Nevertheless it thrusts upon every concerned Christian the responsibility for conscientious analysis of contemporary trends in the definition of Christian mission. And such analysis should lead to effective engagement in Christian witness throughout the world today.

The purpose of this present study, attempted in the course of a guest lectureship at Fuller Theological Seminary, has been to focus on these trends and on the world situation as they affect our Christian calling. Perhaps, under the blessing of God, these chapters may contribute to a greater awareness of the problems we face and may awaken in us a greater sense

---

[1] The reader is referred to the Bibliography.

of concern. If Christians are helped to bear a more conscientious and faithful witness for our Lord, the effort of presenting these lectures in printed form will have been amply rewarded.

II

ASSAULTS UPON THE
CHRISTIAN FAITH

A FAMILIAR BRAIN-TWISTER DEPICTS THREE MISSIONARIES AND three headhunters standing on the bank of a swollen river. At their feet lies a dugout canoe that will hold only two at a time. Across the raging torrent lies their destination. The missionaries must cross in company with the headhunters but they dare not allow themselves to be outnumbered at any time. The big question is, How do they get across?

Emissaries of the church of Christ face a similar situation as they stand on the banks of the tumultuous waters of today's revolution. They are forced to cross, and they must do it in company with others who give every indication of being ferocious headhunters intent upon their destruction. The analogy is a real one, and the problem is complicated by the fact that modern Christians not only have to watch out for their enemies but also must deal with differences that exist among themselves. As a matter of fact, it may not even be quite clear who are the headhunters and who the mission-aries!

Any study of the mission of the church and her evangelistic task in the world of today must consider the pressures or assaults that come from without and the tensions that exist within. This is necessary both for a definition of mission and for a program of action.

The contemporary threat to Christianity from without comes from three main directions. These are: (1) the assault of modern scientific secularism upon the fundamental pre-suppositions of Christianity; (2) the challenge posed by the resurgence and expansion of the major ethnic religions and by the prolific spread of modern cults; and (3) the frontal attack of world communism.

When Julian Huxley says that "religion of the highest and fullest character can co-exist with a complete absence of belief in revelation in any straightforward sense of the word, and of belief in that kernel of revealed religion, a personal God,"[1] he is but expressing the attitude of contemporary scientific secularism toward the fundamental presuppositions of Christianity. Since such secularism admits no evidence that cannot be tested and proved by scientific measure, the super-natural must be ruled out. Hence, it is reasoned, the existence of a personal Supreme Being and the ideas of creation and revelation with all that they involve cannot be accepted by modern men of intellectual maturity and integrity. And the traditional dogmatic definitions of Christianity must give way to more "honest" and "mature" (scientific) interpretations of the universe and of human existence. Only if Christianity is divested of these traditional claims can it continue to be useful to man as a religion, we are told by today's brand of secularism.

The impact of this assault is reflected in much of the writing of contemporary theologians and in such popular treat-ments as Bishop John A. T. Robinson's *Honest to God.*

Secularism's assault is therefore directed against the super-

---

[1]Julian Huxley, *Religion without Revelation* (N.Y.: New American Library, 1959), p. 13.

natural character of Christianity. It concerns itself with the question of the existence of a personal God, who as Creator, Ruler, and Redeemer is present and active in the universe. Christian mission and witness today must be conceived and discharged in full awareness of this secularist rejection of the supernatural and in convincing answer to the basic question it has raised.

Another challenge is posed by the resurgence of traditional non-Christian religions and the spread of new sects. One of the most phenomenal is the Soka Gakkai sect in Japan. From twenty thousand followers in 1945, it has mushroomed to approximately fifteen million adherents today. This is merely the most dynamic of Japan's countless non-Christian religions. They, and others like them around the world, constitute a challenge that is directed not so much against the supernaturalism of Christianity as against its claim to uniqueness and universality. In the shrines of certain of the other faiths, room can be made for the Christian concept of God, even for Jesus Christ and for the Christian myths (so-called) and traditions. The question is one of coexistence. What this revival of religion is saying is that there are other ways of salvation and other roads to God. In effect, the existence of these religions and their new vitality represent a challenge to the Christian claim of uniqueness and to Christianity's right to supplant all other religions — and this in a day when tolerance has become one of the supreme virtues.

The non-Christian religious revival, therefore, challenges the very claims that lie at the heart of the missionary concern of the church of Christ. And as Edmund Perry has said, "For the first time in its own history the Christian faith is on the brink of a decisive encounter with the other major religious systems of the world which are now determined to define the encounter in their own terms."[2]

Impressed by the vitality of these faiths, many modern leaders and thinkers are expressing the conviction that in this

---

2 Edmund Perry, *The Gospel in Dispute. The Relation of Christian Faith to Other Missionary Religions* (N.Y.: Doubleday, 1958), p. 16.

shrinking planet and emerging one-world civilization there can no longer be any room for competitive religions with their exclusivist claims. Either there must come about, they say, the emergence of a one-world religion as a result of the blending of the better elements of the many, or else the different religions must relinquish their exclusive claims and learn to recognize and relate to each other for the sake of the common good. The nature and implications of this challenge have been dealt with by Lesslie Newbigin.[3] The new attitude of excessive tolerance provides one more reason why the Christian church must make sure of its claims.

Pressures from outside thus have undermined the sense of confidence with which the Christian missionary has gone out to evangelize and conquer the world for Christ. He is now forced to a reexamination of claims that he has always taken for granted. In these days of easy travel and free contact between the races and cultures, he is discovering that it is no light matter to brush aside another's culture and tradition and to present to him the claims of salvation in Christ alone, when his hearer may appear to be equally as refined and just as motivated morally as many so-called Christians. Also, in all honesty and humility, he is forced to recognize the existence of difficult questions concerning the validity of the other man's religion, and the extent of God's redemptive working among vast numbers of non-Christians whose ethnic environment has been such as to make almost humanly impossible a proper understanding of the Christian gospel, particularly when presented in Western dress.

Communism also poses a threat. Dr. Frank W. Price has called the twentieth century "the century of Communist power"[4] in describing its incredible expansion and its assault upon the political, economic, and social structures of the world Like the scientific secularism of the West, communism rejects

---

[3] J. E. Lesslie Newbigin, *A Faith For This One World?*

[4] Frank W. Price, "Christian Presuppositions for the Encounter with Communism," *The Theology of the Christian Mission,* ed. by Gerald Anderson, pp. 158-167.

all supernaturalism. But its challenge to Christianity goes beyond that.

Today in the midst of the want and hunger that the great masses are suffering in Asia, Africa, and Latin America, communism challenges the Christian affirmation that man shall not live by bread alone. One has only to look upon the tide of human misery and be a spectator to the unrest and unhappiness of the masses to recognize that Christianity is not merely facing a problem of communication — that is, a problem of gaining a hearing for the gospel. It faces also the problem of meeting immediate, urgent need, of giving true expression to the gospel it preaches; and its survival depends upon this.

Communism, therefore, not only challenges the theological presuppositions of Christianity as does Western secularism, but in a world of population explosion, of social misery, political strife, and sheer hunger, it challenges the Christian church to be Christian in deed, to express the compassion of Christ in concrete and comprehensible reality. So communism drives us toward a fresh biblical understanding of the Christian mission and function in the world, of social and political responsibility in a day of collectivism, and of the demands and obligations of Christian love toward those who in one sense are enemies and who are nevertheless beloved of God.

The situation is further complicated by deep tensions that exist within the Christian church itself, and an understanding of these is essential for defining and discharging mission in the world of today.

The most obvious evidence of these tensions is the divided state of Christendom. Only an outsider can fully appreciate the extent of our dividedness. We ourselves are so accustomed to our inherited fragmentation that we are scarcely aware of the anomaly presented to non-Christians on local, national, and worldwide levels by the spectacle of differing church bodies existing side by side in utter separation, while each group claims to belong to Christ. This not only brings up questions about the essential unity of the church of Christ, and the relationship between the different members of the body, but it also brings up the important question of testimony. Can a divided church effectively proclaim one gospel and one Lord to the segmented and skeptical world of today?

On the other hand, there are considerations of truth and principle that cannot be dodged. Tragic as the spectacle of a divided Christendom may be, there is an obligation of fidelity to truth which must take precedence over any desire for unity based on mere sentiment or convenience. Just as Israel's rejection or misunderstanding of messianic truth led to the cleavage between the Jews and those who followed Christ, so in every succeeding age deviation from truth has forced upon the professing body of Christ sad but inevitable divisions. The greater tragedy of spiritual failure lies in the needless separation and hostility between those who, despite their different characteristics and convictions, do belong to Christ. It is at this point that Christian testimony stands discredited in the eyes of the world.

But organizational divisions are usually the expression of inner differences of conviction and outlook that run deep and therefore cannot be reconciled with ease. It is primarily in the spheres of biblical interpretation and theological reflection, as Christians respond to the contemporary situation, that the lines are drawn and division takes place. The theological battles of yesterday have given way to the struggle to understand and define Christian truth in light of modern scientific reality and in terms of the contemporary existentialist mood. It is in the context of this inevitable struggle that the tensions between conservatives and liberals, between traditionalists and progressives, must be examined.

At the heart of this struggle, creating the great continental divide that transcends all denominational lines, is the conviction held regarding the source of final authority for Christian belief and life. The acceptance of a divine revelation, fully inspired and wholly authoritative, must be the touchstone for understanding the differences that separate Christians in many aspects of doctrine, ethic, social obligation, and evangelistic methodology.

One other area of tension among Christians should also be

mentioned. Along with the questions of what he believes and the ultimate source of authority for that belief, the Christian is constantly faced with the question of the experience of power. The gift of the Holy Spirit is an essential element of his witness. But the variety of Christian experience has given rise to differing outlooks on the subject. As in past ages of Christian history, Christians are divided again over the experience of power and the forms it may take. The spread of the Pentecostal movement in this century and the recent upsurge of charismatic manifestations have served to focus upon the dynamic essential to mission. But they have also created a tension within the Christian community which needs honestly to be recognized and dealt with.

We come back then to the missionaries and the headhunters in their perilous crossing of the turbulent stream. Once again we are reminded by analogy of the dangers, pressures, and tensions that face the Christian church as it seeks to discover and discharge its sacred mission in the secular world of today. Its ability to cross the troubled waters will depend upon its understanding of its task and the risks involved in the completion of it.

III

CHRISTIAN RESPONSES
TO THE CHALLENGE

ONE OF THE SIGNIFICANT DEVELOPMENTS IN PROTESTANTISM[1] IN the years that have followed World War II has been the remarkable growth of conservative evangelical sentiment, particularly in North America. This has resulted in the emergence of a conservative evangelical force which, in reaction to trends within the "historic" churches, is rapidly developing a life of its own. As against some forty million church members who are linked through their church connections to the National Council of Churches in the United States, there are some twenty-four million members who belong to this conservative wing.

The vigor of this movement is discernible in many different forms, but primarily in its zealous dedication to evangelistic

---

[1] The striking developments and indications of renewal within the Roman Catholic Church and the study of mission going on in that communion are recognized as being of special significance, demanding separate treatment which is not attempted here.

and missionary outreach. This has been expressed in (1) the revival of mass evangelism in traditional patterns, but with the use of modern media and techniques of communication; (2) the rise and development of lay evangelism, stimulated by a host of organizations very loosely related to the organized churches; and (3) an amazing missionary outreach over all the world.

Its comparative strength can be seen from the fact that during recent years, while the number of foreign missionaries sent out by the Division of Foreign Missions of the National Council increased by 4.5 percent, those of the conservative evangelicals increased by 149.5 percent, with a proportionate increase in financial income. As a result, conservative evangelical missionaries from the United States represent a missionary force more than 50 percent larger than that of the historic bodies scattered over the face of the earth. In Latin America the proportion approaches a ratio of three to one.[2]

A superficial analysis of this conservative evangelical response to the challenge of the world's situation would seem to lead to three simple conclusions. First and most obvious, it is evident that the response has been in terms of *action* — evangelistic action. Evangelicals, impressed with a sense of the urgency of the task and the shortness of time, seem to have felt little obligation or inclination to study and reflect upon the precise nature of the modern situation and its demands. The output of conservative literature on the subject is amazingly limited. The entire stress in conservative evangelical circles has been on action. As a result, they can point with some pride to missionary expansion, to mass evangelistic efforts that equal or excel those in any period of Christian history, and to an impressive increase of churches of similar theological conviction in every part of the world.

In the second place, evangelicals have taken a defensive attitude in their theological outlook. In meeting the assaults of the modern world upon the faith, their defense of the source of authority and of an orthodox definition of Christianity has

---

2 Missionary Research Library *Occasional Bulletin,* Dec. 8, 1958, etc.

been considered more important than any new theological insights or any adaptation of their position to the modern age.

Evangelical outreach has been characterized, in the third place, by a tenacious adherence to traditional methods and patterns of church life and work. Both as to message and method, and notwithstanding a readiness to adapt modern media and techniques of communication, the stress has been on continuity with the past, coupled with a certain distrust of involvement with the new.

Evangelical conservatism and zeal in evangelism have provoked considerable criticism. Christians outside of the movement — and therefore perhaps capable of greater objectivity — have pointed to certain deficiencies. Among these are: (1) a zeal that in some cases confuses proselytism with true witness or evangelism; (2) a stress on individual piety that emphasizes the conventional standards of the group and neglects to grapple in practical ways with the ethical implications of the gospel as they bear upon the complexities of modern society; (3) a dogmatism in doctrinal matters that seems to foster spiritual arrogance and is unnecessarily divisive; (4) a separatism from the world that is often legalistic and pharisaical in spirit; and (5) a superficiality in the presentation of the gospel that contributes largely to the apparent irrelevance of the church in the world today.

These criticisms may surprise and shock evangelicals, who rightly resent the popular caricatures of the fundamentalist movement. The danger, of course, is that in rejecting unfair misrepresentations, they may fail to accept — as from the Lord — that which is valid in the criticisms leveled against them. This is one of the reasons why a careful study of the mission of the church needs to be made today, particularly by those who are concerned that the Christian church of tomorrow shall remain true to "the faith which was once for all delivered to the saints."

On the other hand, it is important that the full value of the conservative contribution be recognized. As the emissaries of the church of Christ face the torrent of mankind's conflicting opinions, the voice of the conservative cries out: "We must be faithful to revealed truth. And we must obey the Great Commission." In the area of mission and witness, this insistence on faithfulness and obedience may well be the most important contribution made by the conservative evangelical to the cause of Christ.

It is of equal importance that we seek to understand what the so-called mainstream of Protestantism is seeking to say. We can grapple with the problems that face us and hope for an evangelical apologetic and corrective only if we understand historic Protestantism's response to the contemporary pressures and tensions. Only thus can we expect to contribute to the fulfillment of the church's true mission in these climactic days.

Of special importance is the study that has been carried out by the Division of Studies of the World Council of Churches. Centering on the theme "The Word of God and the Church's Missionary Obedience," this study, in which World Council scholars all over the world have participated, has resulted in the writing of two books.[3] In these, as well as in the bulletins put out by the WCC Division of Studies, we may presume to hear the voice of traditional Protestantism.

In his study of the biblical basis of Christian mission as seen in the writings of modern theologians, Johannes Blauw carefully surveys the Old and New Testament Scriptures. This survey (pp. 15-103) serves as a foundation for a summary (pp. 104-136) which culminates in a definition of the mission of the church based on I Peter 2:9-10. It is followed by a series of valuable footnotes (pp. 137-172).

In the Old Testament, Blauw traces the history of God's call of a special people and of the purpose behind it. From the very beginning the choice of Israel has a missionary motivation. "The election of Israel," says Blauw, "is a matter of divine initiative which has as its goal the recognition of God by all nations over the whole world. The way to this goal is the theocracy of Israel; the means is Israel's separation from other peoples."[4]

---

3 Johannes Blauw, *The Missionary Nature of the Church;* D. T. Niles, *Upon the Earth.*

4 Blauw, *op. cit.,* p. 24.

Turning to the New Testament, Blauw notes first its continuity with the Old in its universal outlook. At the same time,
a discontinuity with the Old is recognized. Christ's teaching
regarding the kingdom, his choice of a new priesthood (the
apostles and disciples), his forming of a new body — the
church — are all part of a new order.

He concludes then that a "theology of mission" cannot be
otherwise than a "theology of Church."

> In Christ a new creation has arisen. The world must *hear*
> from the community of Christ that the new world of God has
> begun. The chosen race, the royal priesthood, the holy nation,
> the people of God's own possession is itself the beginning of
> this new world. And the "loud proclamation" of the Church
> is a continuation of the calling of God. Just as God's sending
> of the Son continues in the sending of the Spirit and the
> sending of the community into the world (John 20:21), so
> the calling of God continues in the proclamation of the
> Church.[5]

It is upon this definition of the missionary nature of the
church that D. T. Niles then proceeds to consider the task
of the church in the world of today. *Upon the Earth* is in some
ways more interesting and stimulating than its companion
volume, yet more difficult to follow. It raises certain questions
and in the end may leave the reader with a sense of disappoint-
ment. Announced on its dust jacket as "the most thorough re-
thinking of the Christian mission that has been done in recent
years," it leaves the conservative evangelical, at least, with the
impression that more thinking needs to be done — and that it
needs to be more definitely anchored in Scripture.

The central thesis of Niles' book is that "the earth is the
true correlate of the Gospel and that, therefore, the goals and
the problems of this earthly life in all their complexity are the
true addresses of the missionary endeavor."[6]

It is from this perspective that Niles focuses upon the missionary enterprise (missions) today and seeks to bring it into
line with the true goals and biblical purpose for which the

---

5 *Ibid.,* p. 133.
6 Niles, *op. cit.,* p. 12.

church exists. Modern "missions" therefore throughout the book are seen as a part of the "mission" of the church, historically necessary but not necessarily correct. The church is seen in terms of her missionary calling alone, and hence the underlying assumption is that "the church is mission." The task of today as conceived by Niles is to effect the needed reform of church and missionary structures, together with their patterns of work, in order to make possible the proper relation to the world.

It becomes important, then, to understand exactly what is meant by "mission." The church, Niles implies, must be defined as mission; it is an activity in the world, rather than a company saved from the world. He states it this way: "The Church's mission is to be the people of God everywhere — in every situation, in every land and nation, in all areas of life." Hence the "task of evangelism is the task of bringing the Gospel to those who have not heard it, of building the Christian community within a people among whom such a community does not exist, of maintaining the Christian witness amidst current problems and tensions in all areas of human relationships, of exerting the pressure of the Christian way of life on those who do not yet accept it."[7]

These and other quotations might be cited to reveal the concept of mission that Niles presents. If we have understood him correctly, Christian mission as Niles defines it can be summed up as that witness and involvement in every phase and problem of the world's earthly life whereby the Lordship of Jesus Christ is proclaimed for all peoples and societies, in the knowledge that by his death and resurrection he has reconciled the entire universe unto himself. Therefore, he says, all human activity now contributes to the establishment of that eternal kingdom which Christ will consummate at the end of time and of which his church is presently the firstfruits.

The implications of such a definition of mission become clear as the subject is developed. Blauw and Niles furnish a needed corrective for churches whose unconscious reason for

7 *Ibid.,* p. 75.

existence has become self-aggrandizement and self-perpetuation. They rightly call the churches to come out from their pharisaical isolationism and pseudopietism and become — as Christ meant them to be — true salt and light *in* the world. They correctly demand that our eyes be opened to the universal horizons of God's redemptive purposes and that we focus upon portions of his revealed Word that, in our particularist bias, we have tended to ignore. In the midst of an anguished humanity in desperate straits, they rightly echo the Lord's cry for attending to justice and mercy — those weightier demands of the law to feed the poor and heal the sick — which a proselytistic zeal is ever prone to. evade. And they raise questions about our missionary structures and programs that ought to be raised.

At the same time such a definition of mission seems to be based on conclusions not fully warranted by the whole of revealed truth — at least as traditionally understood. According to this concept of mission, election seems to be defined solely in terms of service rather than salvation. "Once the leaven is mixed with the dough," says Niles, "it has no other function except to lose its identity."[8] That this function is an essential element in election cannot be denied. It is also necessary to keep in mind that the church is constituted and exists solely by grace apart from any human righteousness or merit. But is this definition of election wholly correct? Has God chosen a people solely as an instrument, or has he predestinated his own unto salvation and sanctification and fellowship with himself? Certainly such Scriptures as Ephesians 1:4-6; I Peter 1:3-5; Romans 8:26-30; John 15:15; Hebrews 2:9-15; and I John 1:3-4 — to mention but a few — would seem to suggest that the intent of election goes beyond that of mere instrumentality, important as this function may be.

If election is only for service, then the moral transformation and perfection of the individual Christian is a matter of no great importance. This seems to be Niles's point of view. "To put it crudely," he says, "the heart of Christianity is not con-

8 *Ibid.*, p. 103.

cern for the soul but concern for the world."[9] And again, "The rightful insistence on the necessity of personal conversion and commitment to Jesus Christ has in large measure given rise to the impression that salvation is an individual matter. 'I believe and am saved.' In terms of the New Testament perspective this is a distortion. The truth is that when I believe, I find myself involved in God's work of salvation. My own salvation is part of that work."[10] And once again: "Salvation can be for me only a call to follow Jesus in His saving ministry."[11]

Illustrative of this concept is the exposition given of Paul's encounter with the Philippian jailor. Niles renders the jailor's cry for help thus: " 'Sirs, what must I do to be safe?' — to be safe in the morning when the magistrates come." Niles seems to conceive of the jailor's salvation as consisting merely in deliverance from the fear of the magistrates, or as confident daily living in the world. "Safe, whatever happens — that is salvation,"[12] he says.

In dealing with the subject of individual salvation it is necessary to keep in mind that no man lives unto himself, that growth and fellowship and service and witness are necessarily experienced in relationship to community and society. But to define salvation as participation in the collective ministry and service of the church, is to ignore that vast portion of Scripture in which salvation is defined in terms of the new birth and sonship, or moral perfection and fellowship with God, and which sees the salvation of one single soul as of infinite value in the eyes of God (Luke 15:7, 10).

The accuracy of Niles's definition of the relation of the church to the world is also to be questioned. We have already recognized the corrective it contains. But it would seem that in the effort to correct admitted failures, it recommends a swing in the opposite direction that is not fully in keeping with the teaching of Scripture. Throughout his book, Niles

9 *Ibid.*, p. 52.
10 *Ibid.*, p. 106.
11 *Ibid.*
12 *Ibid.*, p. 49.

has stressed the church's responsibility to be light and salt in the world, "to be the people of God everywhere — in every situation, in every land and nation, in all areas of life";[13] to make the gospel relevant "by entering fully into the life of the world";[14] "to exert a peculiar pressure on the forms of common life."[15]

But what are the full implications of these statements? Do they call the church to an identification with the world that fails to take into account the evident dualism of the Bible and its revelation of the enduring hostility that separates the world from God in the organizing and ordering of human life and welfare on the earth?

Niles sees two movements currently under way in the world, the Christian witness and the secular endeavor to provide for an abundant life, both of which are instruments for the working out of God's purposes among the nations. These must be related, he says.

> *God's design is one humanity.* A secular side of this design is being realized in the work of the United Nations Organization and its several agencies. *God's design is a new creation.* A secular side of this design is being fulfilled through scientific research, increased technical efficiency, the application of atomic power for peaceful purposes, and similar developments. *God's design for man is abundant life.* A secular side of this design is the goal of such organizations as the World Health Organization, the Food and Agriculture Organization, and the World Bank. *God's design for man is life in community* — characterized by freedom and justice, and the wealth of human association. A secular side of this design is the concerns of the Security Council and of the World Court, and the various programmes of U.N.E.S.C.O. The missionary enterprise is not an enterprise apart from or even alongside these secular movements. It is essentially also a secular movement which gives to these other movements their true place and perspective in the working out of God's total design. The missionary enterprise and the ecumenical movement must

---

13 *Ibid.*, p. 75.
14 *Ibid.*, p. 117.
15 *Ibid.*, p. 78.

provide the means of interlocking man's eternal destiny and his present life, of interweaving the life of the people of God which is the Church with the lives of men as men in the world.[16]

How is this to be reconciled with the clear statements of Scripture that reveal the persistence of hostility to God on the part of organized human society, that reveal the fundamental difference in character between the kingdom of God and the kingdoms of men, and that pronounce the word of judgment upon the latter? The Christian's involvement in the world and his relationship to the world must be governed by the realities of anticipated judgment as well as of hoped-for mercy in God's dealings with the world at the end. In all love and truth, with God's purpose for ultimate blessing of all peoples in mind, the Christian must be both the fragrance of life unto life and the savor of death unto death.[17] This solemn truth must govern the Christian in all his relations and responsibilities to the world.

The reader of *Upon the Earth* is bound to be impressed by the note of conditional universalism which runs through it and which seems to form the major presupposition upon which the definition of Christian mission is based.

It is introduced in a graphic way in the opening dialogue of the book. "A person viewing the missionary task is as it were standing at a cross-roads where three roads meet and cross. The signboard of the first road reads — All men, the whole world, the whole creation, all things. The signboard of the second road reads — Each man, he who believes, he that is chosen. The signboard of the third road reads — The part shall consecrate the whole. The significance of the junction is that here these three roads meet."[18]

Just what takes place at the junction is made clear later on. We quote at length because of the importance of the subject. Says Niles:

---

16 *Ibid.*, p. 268. Italics his.
17 See II Cor. 2:14-17.
18 Niles, *op. cit.*, p. 18.

There are those who insist that no genuine and urgent conviction about the mission of the Church is possible unless
one is able to say positively: Some will be saved and others
will be damned ... (John 3:18). ... Surely there are a series of
exclamation marks which the New Testament puts in face
of too categorical an answer to the question raised! First, is
there any real substance in the claim that God's great design
for His whole creation will be fulfilled unless that claim includes the assertion that it will be fulfilled for each person?
(Luke 15:4.) Second, where in the New Testament is the span
of this earthly life set out as the measure of the limits of
God's grace? Third, who shall say that the evangelistic presentation of Jesus Christ will necessarily be for anyone, who hears
that presentation, the moment of his decision for Jesus Christ?
Does not the Master offer Himself for acceptance by some of
His children (Matt. 25:31f.) in ways and forms that are of
His own choosing and which may not ever carry the label
"Christian"?[19]

Niles seems to recognize the conditions laid down for
response to the gospel. "The New Testament," he says, "will
allow no diminution of the fact that there is only one Saviour
— Jesus Christ (Acts 4:12) ; nor will it allow any compromise
of the fact that salvation is by faith in Him (Rom. 1:16) ."[20]
He adds that "there will be no change in God's demands of
men even at the last. No man need go astray or waste his
opportunities for godly decision by hoping that at the end
there will be a sentimental letting down of standards on the
part of God."[21]

But how, in the face of these unalterable conditions, a
universal salvation is possible, Niles does not explain. Nor
does he ever seem to indicate any awareness of the fact that a
vindication of the divine goodness on the basis of the terms
he sets forth would ultimately require an absolute and unconditional universal salvation and not the limited and conditional salvation for which he holds out hope. He merely
contents himself with stating that it is not our problem, that

19 *Ibid.*, pp. 92-93.
20 *Ibid.*, p. 93.
21 *Ibid.*, pp. 94-95.

"Faith and Hope jump from the redeemed community to the redemption of all things, a jump which is possible only because the in-between situation of unbelief is comprehended within the mystery of God's plan of salvation."[22]

Niles makes copious use of New Testament references, but he consistently refuses to deal with the hard teaching of Scripture — particularly of the sayings of Christ — on the subject. Therefore he holds out an uncertain, conditional, inconsistent form of universal hope. His assumption is that God's eternal purpose will not be accomplished unless in the end all men and all things are reconciled to him. Niles's hope depends upon supporting inferences such as that man's inheritance as provided by God (Rom. 8:17; Eph. 1:18; I Pet. 3:7) belongs to the whole family and is indivisible;[23] and that the firstfruits sanctify the whole.[24]

This universalistic interpretation given to the New Testament underlies the new definition of Christian mission and determines Niles's concept of the message, goals, and methods of the church's witness in the world. From such an understanding of the New Testament arises also that scarcely concealed disdain for the traditional historic Christian definition of salvation and human destiny, for Christian piety, and for the traditional goals and methods of evangelism.[25]

So much for the studies that have culminated in Blauw's summary of *The Missionary Nature of the Church* and Niles's application of its mission, *Upon the Earth.* Bishop Newbigin has indicated in the foreword to the latter book that these writings represent only a stage in the thinking of the leaders of the Division of Studies of the World Council of Churches, and are not final, but are submitted in the hope that they will stimulate further thought, and raise questions that will help the church find its true vocation in the world today.

Our study of these writings has had as its aim to understand and profit by the insights uncovered in this search for

---

22 *Ibid.,* p. 71.
23 *Ibid.,* pp. 89-90, 105-107.
24 *Ibid.,* p. 75.
25 *Ibid.,* see pp. 176, 198.

a timely and acceptable redefinition of mission. But we must in all conscience state that it has brought us to the conviction that the definition advanced in them does not fully and accurately represent the teaching of the New Testament on the subject. Such a definition will only serve to sidetrack and divert the church of Christ from discovering and discharging its true mission in the world of today. It is this failure to reflect accurately the New Testament teaching that makes necessary a continued search for a clear understanding of the biblical definition and patterns of the church's mission today.

BIBLICAL BASES OF MISSION

IV

CHRISTIAN MISSION DEFINED

IN THE VARIED RESPONSES OF PROTESTANT CHRISTENDOM TO contemporary theological pressures and tensions, we have noted two tendencies. One is the trend to define the function and mission of the church in such a way as to emphasize its universalistic outreach, to stress its primary application to this earthly existence, and to promote mainly its communal or collective character. Such a concept of church mission is critical of the traditional structures and forms of Christian life and witness; implicit in it is the advocacy of radical reform.

At the other extreme is a conservative reaction that would define the Christian mission merely in terms of an unbalanced particularism, with strong stress on tradition and individualistic other-world salvation. Often employing an archaic vocabulary that is devoid of meaning to the present generation, it has sometimes seemed to reflect stereotyped attitudes and postures that have become the easy victims of caricature. This extreme speaks in terms of "souls" rather than "persons." In its desire to remain unspotted by the world, it has tended to isolate itself from the mainstream of human struggle. It is intensely

43

traditionalist by nature, seeking often to conserve and per-
petuate institutions and concepts regardless of their current
value or degree of scriptural validity.

In the light of these differing responses, we sense the urgent
need for an understanding of Christian mission that is firmly
anchored in Scripture and at the same time cognizant of the
needs and opportunities of the day. So we ask the questions
that have been uppermost in recent years. What does the
Christian church actually exist for? What is its task and function in modern society and in the world of today? And what
is the Christian's *raison d'être?*

Turning to the Bible for answers to our questions, we are
reminded that its central theme is redemption. God, who in
his sovereign wisdom created man, endowing him with moral
faculties and freedom, and who, in the inexorable outworking
of the laws of his universe, permitted man's fall, has also provided for his restoration. And the Bible is the inspired revelation of that provision. The whole span of earthly history is
the story of the outworking of God's redemptive purpose —
in keeping with the laws, both natural and moral, which he
built into the universe, and with full respect for man's freedom. The character of both the beginning and the end of time
is briefly and partially disclosed in Scripture, but its main
portions spell out the centuries-long story of salvation. And it
is in this process, described in the pages of the Old and New
Testaments, that we perceive the divine objective that determines our mission in the world.

That redemption centers in Jesus Christ, through whom is
both revealed and accomplished God's eternal purpose "which
he set forth in Christ as a plan for the fulness of time, to unite
all things in him, things in heaven and things on earth" (Eph.
1:9-10; see also Eph. 3:9-11; Phil. 2:8-11; Col. 1:12-19; Heb.
2:9-11; and I Cor. 15:24-28).

It is in the light of Jesus Christ that the whole story of
humanity falls into a clear pattern. This is the theological
foundation upon which mission is defined and evangelism
carried out. It is in Jesus, both Son of man and Son of God,
that God reveals the ideal which from the beginning he has

had for man. Here is the real man in perfect relationship to the Father and to his fellow men. Here is true creaturehood. This is what man can be in the universe in which God placed him. Therefore, in the person of Jesus Christ, man glimpses God's design and desire — to restore the image, to bring him to the stature of the fullness of Christ (Col. 3:10; Eph. 4:13; Rom. 8:29; I Cor. 15:49).

But before such a design can be realized, because we are twisted and perverted by wrongdoing, we must behold Jesus also as "the lamb of God that takes away the sin of the world." We understand therefore that his coming to the world involves the mystery of divine judgment and mercy that leads to the cross and resurrection and that shall finally culminate in his coming in glory and judgment. The "redemption that is in Christ" only becomes effectual through his death and resurrection, and thus gives rise to the simple gospel proclamation of the apostles, "that Christ died for our sins in accordance with the scriptures, that he was buried, that he was raised on the third day in accordance with the scriptures" (I Cor. 15: 3-4).

After Jesus' ascension, in the unfolding of his teaching and in the completed working of the Holy Spirit, his disciples come to an understanding of something of what redemption includes. In their experience, it begins with the forgiveness of sins and the consciousness of a new life (John 1:12-13; 3:6-8); it involves incorporation into his body, and the reception of the Holy Spirit to perfect God's life in them and to equip them for service and witness in the fellowship of his church.

Salvation then, in biblical terms, is rooted in the transformation of each individual in order that he may be thus incorporated into the family of God. It is not merely a call to service and a partnership in action; it is first a call to repentance and faith, to sonship and to a new life, marked by holiness and obedience, worship and fellowship. No longer servants but friends (John 15:15); no longer servants but sons (Gal. 4:1-6) — this is what salvation means.

God's purpose in redemption begins with the renewal of the individual man, through which he is brought back to proper relationship with God and with his fellow men. This is God's will for every citizen of his kingdom. Mission and service therefore, while linked to the outworking of God's salvation, are subsequent to it. "Marvel not that I said unto thee," Jesus tells Nicodemus, "ye must be born again" (John 3:7). But birth is the first sign of ongoing life. Salvation therefore involves also mission and service — not for some but for all. "We are his workmanship," says St. Paul, "created in Christ Jesus unto good works, which God hath before ordained that we should walk in them" (Eph. 2:10).

This brings us to the subject of human instrumentality in God's mission.

We are able to comprehend in some measure the love that causes God to seek the salvation of the creature whom he has created. We behold that love manifested in the sacrifice of his Son. This we can understand. It is more difficult, however, to fathom why he should accord to human instrumentality a part in the outworking of redemption.

Our consideration of the Christian mission must therefore lead us in all honesty to the question: Why, if God's purpose was the salvation of *all* peoples, did he limit his saving activity to *one* people — Israel? And why has he now limited his saving activity to a people (his church) who, because of their human traits and frailties, are incapable of giving to all the world the light it so desperately needs? These are difficult questions, but the fact is that throughout human history God has chosen to reveal himself redemptively through human instruments.

In the scriptural records these instruments are seen to be Israel in the Old Testament, and the church in the New, as Johannes Blauw brings out so ably in *The Missionary Nature of the Church*. But it is important to note two truths: (1) that God's purposes for and through his people are ever accomplished through the instrumentality of individuals and through saving remnants or committed minorities. This is due not only to a natural need for human leadership, but also to the human pride and disobedience which continually result in the failure of God's people as a whole to fulfill their mission. (2) In spite of this failure, however, God does not abandon his people. He will visit them in judgment and chastisement; he will call in others for the accomplishment of his purpose, but he will fulfill his purpose through them in the end. Israel will be supplanted by the church, and even the church will fail (Rom. 9-11); nevertheless God remains faithful to his covenants; he cannot deny himself.

The Old Testament is seen then as the historic record not only of a choice but of the failure of an instrument — a failure whose full nature and extent does not become clear until Christ's time. But what stands out in this history is the fact that it is never the nation as a whole, but its concerned individuals and its committed minorities, so often persecuted and killed, who in effect do the work of God and accomplish his will.

It is to Abraham as an individual that the promise is given; it is Moses alone in the desert, Samuel in the still hours of the night, David in the sanctuary, Daniel in the prayer chamber, Ezekiel among his brethren in exile, Nehemiah in the palace of the Gentile king — and a host of other lonely, burdened individuals to whom God's will is made known. Their mission is discharged through the believing minorities that respond to their voices and claim the promises of God — Moses' young men, Gideon's three hundred, David's four hundred, the sons of the prophets, and Nehemiah's builders on the wall.

In any study of Christian mission and of evangelistic strategy it is important to keep these points in mind.

In the New Testament there is a further disclosure of God's use of human instrumentality. As Blauw[1] has pointed out, a new community is called by Christ in contrast to Israel. While this new instrumentality is to fulfill all the Old Testament covenants and predictions, yet it is also something radically new. It is in the light of this new situation created by the coming of the Messiah and the setting aside of Israel, the introduction of a new covenant and the establishment of a new

---

[1] Blauw, *The Missionary Nature of the Church*, p. 85.

missionary community, that we perceive the terms of mission for this present age.

In continuity with the Old Testament teaching, the New Testament revelation nevertheless involves radical changes which are worthy of note: (1) As against the former choice of *one* separate people, Israel, the choice is now made of representatives of *all* peoples indiscriminately, but "in Christ" (I Cor. 1:26-28; Acts 10:15, 28; 11:17-18; and Gal. 3:26-28). (2) As against dependence upon a select officialdom for the work of God, choice is made of the common people, and the significance of the choice lies not in the selection of a new dynasty of leaders to replace the old, but in the choice of the people themselves. Though the principle of leadership is not discarded, henceforth leadership is to be interpreted in terms of servanthood (Matt. 10:24; Luke 6:40, etc.). The end of this New Testament process of choice is that the people of God, indwelt by the Spirit of God, may fulfill the mission of God (Eph. 4:12, etc.).

(3) As against the mission to *be* a separate people among the nations, thus testifying to the truth of a holy God, the call now is to *go out* among the nations to *preach* the message of salvation and thus testify to a sovereign Lord. Both the *go* and the *preach* need to be emphasized, and the one kept always in relation to the other. There is no authority for dispersion in the world unless it is accompanied by the preaching of the gospel; there can be no true preaching of the gospel except in the context of the world and in outreach to all the nations.

Therefore, the essential mission of the church of Christ for which it has been equipped by the Holy Spirit is to proclaim the good news of salvation to every creature in all the world and to attest the reality and power of the gospel through the holy lives and genuine love of its members, their devoted service to mankind everywhere, and their patient endurance of suffering. The church fulfills this mission so that men may be led to acknowledge Jesus Christ as Lord and Savior and thus be incorporated into the fellowship and service of his church, while it gives faithful warning of coming judgment to the nations in the sure expectancy of his return to reign.[2]

In the following chapters we shall try to understand more clearly the terms and implications of the Christian mission. For the moment we have sought to focus upon a definition of mission which, in spite of its deficiencies, at least furnishes a yardstick by which the task can be measured and the lines of Christian action determined. The value of this definition will depend, of course, upon the extent of its fidelity to the Word of God.

---

[2] John 16:7-11; 20:22-23; Acts 1:8; 2:1-4; Luke 24:46-48; Acts 10:34-43; 20:20-21; I Cor. 15:1-4; Matt. 28:18-20; I Cor. 1:17-21; Acts 1:8; Rom. 1:5; 15:26; II Cor. 4:1-7; I Pet. 2:9; Titus 2:11-14; John 13:35; Col. 3:12-15; I Cor. 13; Matt. 5:13-16; Matt. 10:18-25; Phil. 1:29; 3:10; I Pet. 4:12-19; I Cor. 12:13; Eph. 2:11-22; Titus 2:13; I Thess. 4:14-17.

V

CHRIST AS A PATTERN OF MISSION

THIS IS THE DAY OF THE MASSES — OF MASS PRODUCTION, MASS psychology, mass communications, and mass movements. We have been reminded recently by a Russian writer that the reign of numbers was brought to an end by the coming of the Son of man. In his great novel *Dr. Zhivago,* Boris Pasternak compares the two great miracles of the Old and New Testaments. In the first is depicted the dramatic, spectacular crossing of the Red Sea; in the second, the quiet, private, almost unperceived birth of a child in a manger.

"What an enormously significant change!" exclaims Pasternak. He goes on to ask, "How did it come about that an individual human event, insignificant by ancient standards, was regarded as equal in significance to the migration of a whole people?"

His conclusion is that a profound change had been introduced into the world — a change that spelled the end of all great human empires like Rome, of all tyrannies of the masses over the individual. "The reign of numbers was at an end," he said; "The duty, imposed by armed force, to live unanimously as a people, as a whole nation, was abolished ... replaced by the doctrine of individuality and freedom. Individual human life became the life story of God and its contents filled the vast expanses of the universe."[1]

Such a reaction from one who died a victim of modern tyranny is a needed reminder of a scriptural truth that is in danger of being forgotten even in our Western world. The whole history of God's work of redemption is made up of the call of individual men and women in the midst of the people for whose sake they are called and situated. Bible history is biographical — the story of men like Moses, Joshua, and David. God reveals himself as the God of individual men — of Abraham, Isaac, and Jacob. The climax of Bible history, as Pasternak has reminded us, is reached in the coming of one man — the man Christ Jesus.

Christ's place in the divine history is set forth by the author of the epistle to the Hebrews in two significant statements:

> God, who gave to our forefathers many different glimpses of the truth in the words of the prophets, has now, at the end of the present age, given us the truth in the Son. (Heb. 1:1-2, Phillips trans.)

> Therefore, when Christ enters the world, he says: Sacrifice and offering thou wouldest not, But a body didst thou prepare for me. (Heb. 10:5, Phillips trans.)

Paul gives testimony to the strategic value of the individual in the plan of God by the significant words: "For as by *one* man's disobedience many were made sinners, so by the obedience of *one* shall many be made righteous" (Rom. 5:19, KJV). His own sense of individual responsibility and mission find eloquent expression in the words, "For this cause I Paul, the prisoner of Jesus Christ for you Gentiles. . ." (Eph. 3:1, KJV).

Christian mission in the Bible is defined in terms of individual calling and endowment and of individual service on behalf of and through a people. In demonstration of this

---

[1] Boris Pasternak, *Dr. Zhivago* (N.Y.: Pantheon, 1958), p. 412.

truth, the Bible brings us through the life stories of number-
less (but not nameless) men of God in olden times up to the
Son of man, on whom centers all the light of sacred story and
who, in addition to being the author and finisher of our faith,
is also the perfect pattern of the divine mission.

Individuality and endowment are both essential to mission
— hence the significance of the words, "a body hast thou prepared me." Here is expressed the truth of the incarnation,
which embodies for every disciple, as it did for Jesus Christ
himself, the basic principle that underlies the discharge of all
Christian mission.

The historic accounts of Christ's birth are found in the
Gospels of Matthew and Luke. It is John who brings out the
eternal significance of that birth. Its mystery and wonder are
summed up in the words, "and the Word became flesh and
dwelt among us" — words that have tugged at human hearts
down through the ages.

Better than any other, they represent the divine answer to
the difficult and humanly impossible question of the *how*
of revelation and redemption. The ambassador of Jesus Christ
who has attempted to proclaim the gospel in clear terms in
the midst of the multitude and has encountered incomprehen-
sion and indifference, begins to understand what it means to
grapple with the problems the divine mind must have faced
in the communication of his redemption to mankind. Such
is the experience of the missionary in a foreign land.

One of the scenes we shall never forget took place some
time ago in the baseball stadium of San Juan, Puerto Rico. It
was Billy Graham's first visit to that island and his one
appearance in that city. The stands were packed, and thou-
sands more were spread over the playing field. It was raining
that night, and to add to the difficulties the public address
system was not functioning properly. In such a setting, with
the rain slanting down on them, the evangelist and his interpreter attempted to present to that great crowd the story
of God's love for man as shown in the death of his Son. How
to make this love of an invisible God real? How to bring to
each one the reality and value of Christ's death for him?

The evangelist, standing tall, cried out: "God loves the world; he loves you!" The interpreter followed in Spanish, "Dios ama al mundo; le ama a usted!" The loudspeakers carried the words across the stadium until the sound bounced back unevenly from nearby buildings, so that the words "God loves you," distorted, twisted, and hardly distinguishable, were sounding in the night air from every direction. Under such circumstances one is suddenly made aware of the vast difficulty of truly communicating such a message at all. It is, as Tom Allan has reminded us, the problem of trying to describe a two-dimensional world to those who live in a world of only one dimension. But the amazing thing that night in Puerto Rico was that somehow, in spite of all the difficulties, the message did get through. As Billy Graham told his audience, the key was God's becoming man, the Word becoming flesh, the truth of God's love made tangible in deeds of love. Thus man is brought to comprehend.

Therefore the incarnation of the Lord Jesus must have a special fascination for his disciples. In this mystery they perceive not only the condescension of redeeming grace but also something of the divine method of redemption. The incarnate Christ becomes the pattern of mission for every disciple. In his movements through life, in his words and deeds, in his relationships to fellow men and to society, are exemplified all the principles of mission.

In the light of this incarnational truth, the disciple looks with new eyes at his own human body, sees its particular physical proportions — its stature, its shape, the ugliness or beauty of it. He acknowledges the serpent of evil coiled within; accepts its baseness and ordinariness; discovers its peculiar gifts and abilities. He sees and accepts all that he is and where he is, and knows himself to be a rod in the hand of God — formed, called, and perfected in infinite love and wisdom by the Father on high. And the instrument he possesses, as he is possessed by his Father, is that body that makes him one with all the human race and enables him to express in flesh and deed, in concrete situations of human life, the love of God and the mystery of grace. Humbly and reverently the disciple utters his Master's words, "A body hast thou prepared me," and hence, "I come to do thy will, O God." When he does, he is in the way of discovering his mission in life.

Moreover the incarnate Word has become to him a pattern for the methods he employs to carry out his mission. In our day we are constantly tempted to stress one method or another, to fix upon one approach above another. We laud mass evangelism to the neglect of personal responsibility, or we stress preaching to the neglect of living, or vice versa. But our Lord's example shows us the way to true balance in these matters.

As we follow Christ's footsteps traced by the Gospel accounts, we note that he moved on three levels of life and ministry. There is first that private inner activity of prayer and communion with his Father — seen in the accounts of the temptation, the nights of lonely prayer vigil in the mountain or desert, the time spent on the Mount of Transfiguration, or at Gethsemane. This element of prayer and communion is never missing throughout the entire span of his earthly life. From this personal devotion to the Father and this life of intercession, Jesus derived his continuous certainty of mission and supernatural power. And the ignorance and poverty of the disciples (yesterday's and today's) in this realm is manifested in such questions and petitions as "Lord, why could not we cast him (the demon) out?" "Lord, teach us to pray." "Increase our faith."

He who in the days of his flesh "offered up prayers and supplications, with loud cries and tears . . . and . . . was heard for his godly fear" has left his disciples a pattern of the life of communion and intercession that is fundamental to effective service and witness. And we who are so concerned to devise techniques and programs of evangelism need first to learn how to pray, to wait upon God, to commune with him in the quiet watches of the night, to know his mind and to become, like him, the anguished ones who plead with God as intercessors on behalf of their fellow men. Does not this example of Christ have much to teach us regarding our mission in life?

Essential to such devotion to the Father and to such a ministry of intercession was the anointing of the Holy Spirit. Here our Lord likewise points the way. Sent into the world and anointed with the Holy Spirit by the Father, so also he sends his disciples and anoints them (John 20:21, 22). The divine Comforter and Intercessor is the secret of Christ's inner strength, and with his coming upon the apostles at Pentecost he brought to all successive generations of Christians the assurance of God's power both in inward devotion and in outward service.

A second level in the life of Jesus is seen in his relationship and dealings with an inner circle of disciples. In this sphere of ministry the essence of his method is found. It is the making of disciples, a process that demands constant individual attention and intimate relationship. But it must be ever kept in mind that Christ's work of making disciples was carried out almost entirely in the midst of his ministry to the multitudes, and that it always had for its goal their eventual ministry to those same multitudes, thus bringing to realization God's ultimate purpose for them.

The first words Christ uttered when he began his public ministry (according to Matthew) were: "Follow me and I will make you fishers of men." The thing to note is that he was after disciples — not sympathizers, nor even converts in the generally accepted sense of the word. Christ began his ministry with the search for disciples, and to the end of that ministry he was still looking for them (Luke 18:22; John 12:26).

How did he pick his men? Without exception they were laymen and unqualified for official positions in Israel's hierarchy. What significance is to be attached to this fact? And what does the gospel record reveal as to their personal qualifications? The biblical accounts make them out to be very ordinary men, typical representatives of mankind itself. Perhaps their chief qualifications are right here: (1) their repre-

sentative ordinariness and (2) their willingness to commit
themselves to discipleship.

A second question to ask is, How did Christ go about
making his followers into disciples? Mark states in a preg-
nant phrase, "And he ordained twelve, *that they should be
with him*" (Mark 3:14). This certainly is one key to Christ's
method of discipling. The call is "Follow *me*." As they observed him in his private life and participated in his public
ministry, and as they accompanied him along the roads of
Palestine, they were formed into disciples.

Another key is his method of teaching. He taught them
"not as the scribes"; he departed from many of the formal
methods of education. He taught his disciples constantly, in
the midst of the everyday situations in which they moved.
It was on-the-job training; and as they experienced the joys
and sorrows of serving the multitudes, of popularity and
rejection, of success and failure, of the daily demands and
constant fellowship with him, he molded and forged them
into disciples.

Making disciples then is the basic pattern and method
laid down by the Lord and followed by the early Christians.
This was the key to Paul's success and the burden of his ex-
hortation to his spiritual son Timothy: "The things that
thou hast heard of me among many witnesses, the same commit thou to faithful men, who shall be able to teach others
also" (II Tim. 2:2).

A third sphere in Christ's life is to be seen in his ministry
among the multitudes. Today there are those who would
question the validity of mass evangelism or decry its value.
But as we follow Christ in the Gospels, we are forced to
recognize that much of his ministry was carried out in the
midst and on behalf of the multitudes. This is the proper
setting and atmosphere for discipling, but it is more — it is
the ultimate goal of Christ's coming. Any reading of the gospel account will reveal how constantly he was surrounded
by masses, and any study of the apostles' witness will show
that they, too, ministered to the multitudes at every opportunity.

Of what did Jesus' work with the multitudes consist? The answer is best found perhaps in the words of Matthew: "And Jesus went about all the cities and villages, teaching in their synagogues and preaching the gospel of the kingdom, and healing every disease and every infirmity" (Matt. 9:35). Preaching ... teaching ... in every town and village — these were the main activities to which he gave himself and which he taught his disciples. And the proof that the Messiah had come was seen in the demonstration of supernatural power over the adversary, in the compassionate healing of the sick, in comfort for the sorrowing and in ministry to the poor.

The gospel account further impresses one with the marked social and ethical concern manifested by Jesus. Here religiousness was not enough. "My mother and my brethren are these which hear the word of God and do it" (Luke 8:21). Justice and mercy in the daily secular lives of the people — these were the concern of the Lord throughout his ministry. The point of this is that Christ's ministry to the multitude is a ministry *to them* and that it takes the form not only of preaching and teaching the kingdom of heaven but of demonstrating and applying its virtues — not as a means of capturing followers but as genuine fulfillment of mission.

It is in this pattern of personal communion with the Father, of disciple-training carried out in the midst of a preaching-teaching-healing ministry to the multitudes that Christ led and instructed his followers. Down through the centuries the people who bear his name have prospered in their witness, have been blessed and have brought blessing to the world to the extent that they have remained faithful to the pattern Christ laid down. Today's Christians who seek to meet the challenge of the world's desperate need can follow no other pattern. "As the Father hath sent me, even so send I you."

VI

THE APOSTOLIC COMMUNITY
AS PATTERN

IN HIS WORK ON THE EXPANSION OF CHRISTIANITY, KENNETH Scott Latourette says of the Christian church of the first century: "Never in so short a time has any other religious faith, or, for that matter, any other set of ideas, religious, political or economic, without the aid of physical force or cultural prestige, achieved so commanding a position. . . ."[1]

The amazing expansion of that first-century church raises a question to which we of the twentieth century must seek the answer. What factors account for this outstanding success in dynamic witness? In this chapter we shall attempt to answer that question.

Taking the order in which Luke relates the story, we must recognize first as most significant the coming of the Holy Spirit upon the disciples according to the promise of the Father and Son. Up to this moment, they had been a small company of ordinary people bound together by their commit-

---

[1] Kenneth Scott Latourette, *The Expansion of Christianity*, I, 112.

ment to Jesus Christ but inhibited by their fear of the authorities and their uncertainty about the future. It was Pentecost that transformed them. The coming of the Holy Spirit alone accounts for the exuberant life and witness described in the subsequent chapters of the Acts of the Apostles.

Any modern search for the secret of dynamic witness must start with a recognition of this factor. Whatever our understanding of the person and work of the Holy Spirit, we must begin here. Our Lord made this clear in his final instructions to the disciples: "You shall receive power when the Holy Spirit has come upon you, and you shall be my witnesses. . . ." The order is clear: first the endowment of power and then the spontaneous witness. And this is the story of the book of Acts.

Throughout this history, the Holy Spirit is omnipresent, baptizing with power, refilling for every emergency, confirming the proclamation of the gospel with signs and wonders, distributing to each disciple his gifts for service, comforting the church, and directly guiding the early Christians in their missionary witness. Everything that characterized the life and action of that primitive community was inspired and generated by him. Any effort to define the Christian mission or to provide for its execution in other terms is to miss the mark and to doom the church of Christ to failure.

The experience of the first-century church must therefore bring the church of the twentieth century to a fresh recognition of the part played by the Holy Spirit in the Christian witness. Avoiding on the one hand the extreme of an unbelief that takes refuge in scholastic rationalizations, and on the other, of a superstitious supernaturalism that ignores the proper conditions of God's working, the church of Christ needs today to recover that experience of the reality and centrality of the Holy Spirit in its midst.

Paul's question to certain Ephesian believers (Acts 19:2), "Did you receive the Holy Spirit when you believed?" is an indication both of the possibility and the difficulty of recognizing palpably the indwelling of the Spirit. But more, it is an eloquent indication of the conviction held by the Apostle

Paul regarding the indispensability of the Holy Spirit. Regardless of its implications, Christians today must face this same question.

The empowering of the Holy Spirit is immediately manifested in the following ways:

(1) Prompt obedience to the Lord's command. Christ had commanded them to preach the gospel to every creature, among all the nations, in the uttermost parts of the earth. This sense of responsibility breathes through the book of Acts. "He commanded us. . . ," says Peter. "We must obey God rather than men. . . ." "We cannot but speak of what we have seen and heard" (Acts 10:42; 5:29; 4:20).

(2) That command was understood to require a verbal communication of the gospel, and this is foremost in the response of apostolic obedience. Today, in reaction to trite and superficial oversimplifications and a cheap huckstering of the gospel, the importance of the verbal communication of the good news is questioned. But we cannot and must not forget its primacy both in the ministry of Christ and in the witness of his first disciples. "It pleased God by the foolishness of preaching to save. . . ," says Paul.

(3) Every disciple, according to the gifts received of the Holy Spirit, participated in the task of making Christ known. Thus the Christian witness is witness in which every Christian participates according to his gifts, in the place in the world in which God has placed him. Deacons are not diverted from witness by other responsibilities; believers are exiled but not deterred from preaching Christ; congregations, like that of Syrian Antioch, launch missionary thrusts; lay people like Priscilla and Aquila convert their homes into centers of evangelistic outreach. This is the picture drawn by Luke of the early Christian disciples.

(4) Prominent in the apostolic testimony is the place given to prayer. Both praise and intercession, individual and collective (Acts 6:4; 2:42; 4:23-31, etc.), are fundamental in that life and witness. Following the example of their Lord, and instructed by the Holy Spirit, the disciples had at last learned

to pray. Consequently their witness was born out of such prayer.

(5) The place of miracles in the apostolic witness must also be recognized. It was not something new to them. The intervention of God in supernatural ways was part of their religious heritage. It was also part of their own experience as they accompanied Jesus throughout his earthly ministry. They had seen him work miracles and they themselves had performed them. And since the Lord had specifically promised this to them before his ascension (John 14:12, etc.) it formed an expected and essential part of their ministry.

The question arises whether these signs and wonders are essential to the preaching of the gospel today. Some have affirmed that they were limited to the period of New Testament revelation and that they ceased shortly thereafter. Others, in reaction to a sterile religious background, have sought in signs and wonders the sense of reality and dynamism that they lacked. Modern Christians tend to divide over this question, and the cleavage is so great that even fellowship and cooperation in evangelism between those who in other essentials of the faith see eye to eye have become almost impossible.

As we note the place of signs and wonders in the early witness, we submit the following observations: (1) Signs and wonders may lead to a type of carnal superstitiousness not honored by God, and are not in themselves infallible proofs of the presence of God in power nor guarantees of Christian perseverance (Matt. 7:22-23; 24:24; II Thess. 2:8-10; Acts 8:9-23). (2) Signs and wonders nevertheless formed a basic part of Christ's ministry, and equally of the life and witness of the apostolic church. Furthermore they have never been entirely missing in the history of the Christian church. They were promised by the Lord as authenticating his presence, as proof of the reality and power of the gospel, and as the means by which divine compassion could express itself in meeting the needs of humanity. Consequently, when the disciples are forbidden by the authorities to preach, and they appeal to the Lord for help, their prayer is that he would enable them to preach the gospel with all boldness: "While thou stretchest out thy hand to heal; and signs and wonders are performed through the name of thy holy servant Jesus" (Acts 4:30) . The effect of these signs is nowhere better demonstrated than in the case of the evangelistic ministry of Philip (not an apostle, by the way), where Luke tells us that "the multitudes with one accord gave heed to what was said by Philip, *when they heard him and saw the signs which he did*" (Acts 8:6) .

If signs and wonders were an essential part of the ministry of the Lord and of his disciples, and if they are inseparably linked to the commission to preach the gospel, the conclusion is unavoidable that they may and should have a place in Christian mission for as long as the Great Commission is in force. As always the disciple will be held in tension between the unbelief that demands signs and wonders (Matt. 16:1-4) and the unbelief that refuses signs (Isa. 7:12) ; as always he will be faced with the necessity of distinguishing between the works that are of God and those which are of man or of Satan (I John 4:1) .

But today, as in apostolic days, we may expect that where God is present, where his gospel is faithfully preached, it will be no unusual thing to see that preaching accompanied by and carried out in an atmosphere of supernatural activity. And more so as the end of this age approaches.

(6) Another characteristic to be noted was the remarkable unity among the early Christians in spite of their great diversity. This unity was maintained only through daily vigilance, as the pleas and exhortations of the apostolic writings clearly indicate. But to a remarkable degree it was there. It was expressed in the prevailing concept that there was only one church or body of Christ. Congregations as well as individual members might vary in gifts, and in their understanding of God's will and experience of his power; they might meet in different places even in one city; there was always the constant struggle to defend the truth against error, to guard against wrong conduct and to preserve order and harmony within the family of God — but they acted in the consciousness that they were only one church. The bear-

ing of this upon the effectiveness of their witness can hardly be overestimated.

This unity was expressed by the warmth of a fellowship that made no distinction between persons. Bread and hearth were shared in generous spontaneity. There in the humble consciousness of undeserved grace, in the honest sharing of common weakness and need, and in the joint pursuit of God-given tasks and goals, they formed closely knit families of spiritual fellowship that drew and welcomed every outsider and every outcast. The effect of this fellowship on the successful carrying out of their mission is beyond exaggeration.

(7) Of equal interest and importance in the effectiveness of the apostolic witness was the relationship of the church to the society in which it moved and to the institutions of its day. The fact that from the beginning the church suffered persecution at the hands of religious and political authorities or of infuriated mobs is clear evidence of the uncompromising character of its witness and its claims. And yet the strong sense of continuity with Israel's tradition and institutions and the apostolic efforts to preserve those links must also be noted. One is impressed as well throughout the book of Acts by the submissive attitude of Christians toward the authority of the Roman Empire under which they lived.

It is obvious to any student of history that the gospel has latent within it the seeds for the social reform and the ideals of freedom and justice which have been achieved in the onward march of human society. It seems equally obvious that the primitive church as a church took no formal steps to express any social concern or effect any social or political reforms. Its hope lay in the coming of the kingdom of heaven, in the rule of its Christ. Whatever the sense of ethical and social responsibility manifested by the early Christians, it was within the realm of God's kingdom, within the compass of the society established by him, that judgment and mercy and righteousness were to reign, that human injustice, cruelty, exploitation, hunger, and want were to be eliminated and that prejudice and inequality were to be rubbed out.

They harbored no illusions about human governments and

society outside of Christ; their only hope lay in the kingdom of God. Their business was to see that his kingdom was presently established in the hearts of men and that its coming in power and majesty was proclaimed to all men. Social action, social justice, and human brotherhood — these were to be demonstrated within the realm of God's kingdom. Their responsibility as salt and light in the world was to demonstrate in everyday life within the fellowship of the kingdom its virtues, and thus to point peoples and nations to the only One and the only sphere where liberty and justice and brotherhood could be the experience of all.

The apostolic church therefore was not ignorant of nor indifferent to its ethical and social responsibility in the world, but rather was acutely aware of the fact that the only hope for the world lay in Christ and his kingdom, and not in the kingdoms of this earth. Therefore they were committed to the one essential task of proclaiming the gospel and so preparing for the coming of Christ's kingdom.

These then are chief characteristics of the early church, produced by the ministry of the Holy Spirit in its midst, which would seem to account for that dynamic life and amazing growth which Latourette has pointed out.

Let us now attempt to summarize. We have sought to point out those aspects of the ministry of Jesus Christ and the witness of his first band of disciples that may serve as patterns of mission and witness for us today. We have seen in the person of Christ the model servant, and we have seen something of his methods in the choice and training of his disciples and the formation of a community in the midst of his ministry to the multitudes. We have followed that small band of disciples after the descent of the Holy Spirit as they moved out in obedience to Christ's command and in imitation of his example. Is it possible now, in a few words, to define the strategy that their example hands down to us? Let us attempt it thus:

The apostolic strategy was to involve every Christian in constant responsible service and witness in every situation of secular and religious life. In these witness-situations, through the teaching ministry of leaders specially gifted and called for the task, a continuous process of disciple-training was carried on. The fruitful end of such activity was a reproductive fellowship and witness on the part of the cells and congregations that make up the one church of Christ.

Discernible in this simple strategy were the following elements: (1) the indispensable operation of the Holy Spirit; (2) the fundamental mediation of prayer; (3) the constant itinerant witness from man to man and from house to house; (4) the opportune proclamation of the gospel to the masses; (5) the intense teaching ministry in the formation of disciples; (6) the outreach of service through healing; and (7) the warmth of fellowship.

This seems to have been the apostolic strategy. The question for us today is whether, in the complexity of modern society and weighed down by the sins that beset us, we can recapture this sense of mission and engage in this joyous fellowship of spontaneous witness. We believe that it is possible and that this is what the future holds out for us. In the following chapters we shall seek to suggest some of the ways and means by which this may be accomplished.

FULFILLING MISSION TODAY

VII

THE CHRISTIAN MARTYR-WITNESS

ONE OF THE BEST DEFINITIONS OF WITNESS WE HAVE SEEN IS THE one given by the ex-communist Whittaker Chambers in his account of the Alger Hiss trial that shook our nation some years ago.

"In time," he addresses his own children, "you will ask yourselves the question: What was my father?"

"I will give you an answer," he goes on. "I was a witness. I do not mean a witness for the Government or against Alger Hiss and the others. Nor do I mean the short, squat, solitary figure, trudging through the impersonal halls of public buildings to testify before congressional committees, grand juries, loyalty boards, courts of law. A man is not primarily a witness *against* something. A witness, in the sense that I am using the word, is a man whose life and faith are so completely one that when the challenge comes to step out and testify for his faith, he does so, disregarding all risks, accepting all consequences."[1]

---

1 Whittaker Chambers, *Witness* (N.Y.: Random House, 1952).

69

It is to this kind of witness that Jesus Christ calls his disciples. It is this kind of witness that the times demand. "When Christ calls a man," observed one modern-day martyr-witness, "He bids him die."[2] To this sort of witness every Christian is summoned.

The fact that today the church and its message seem to many to be largely irrelevant, while at the same time the multitudes are desperately seeking for the solutions to the overwhelming problems that face them, represents an urgent call for a witness that will involve the church in compassionate identification with the world's need while remaining true to its calling and mission. Today's situation therefore demands of the Christian a message that is relevant, a genuine involvement with men and women in their deepest needs, totally apart from what they may ultimately contribute to the church — in short, a witness in depth. The world in the twentieth century stands in desperate need of the Christian of the first century, the martyr-witness who in the final outcome is the only kind of witness that can truly represent the Suffering Servant of God.

The term "witness" was used at first in the New Testament in a forensic sense to refer to the attestation of a fact or event — primarily the death and resurrection of Jesus Christ. From the very beginning it was linked inseparably to the calling — with all its implications and demands — of discipleship.

But witness as demanded by Christ and understood by the apostles was not merely a testimony regarding certain observed events. It involved utter commitment to Christ in light of the significance of those historic events. It was disciple-witness. From the beginning it was made clear that it would result in persecution and death. Hence the call to witness was a call to accept death. Our English word "martyr" derives from the Greek "witness." And the connection is obvious. In a short time, beginning with Stephen, as one after another of the disciples laid down their lives, the term

---

[2] Dietrich Bonhoeffer, *The Cost of Discipleship* (N.Y.: Macmillan, 1959), p. 79.

that described their testimony was linked with the idea of martyrdom. Hence the term "martyr-witness."

As brought out in the New Testament, this concept of martyr-witness is made up of four inseparable elements. They are: (1) the demand for a verbal proclamation; (2) the demonstration of its power and reality in the lives of its proponents; (3) its expression in disinterested service; and (4) its inevitable culmination in suffering and death. Each one of these is an essential part of the witness that the Christian is called upon to give today; together they make up the Christian mission. An emphasis on one or another to the neglect of the rest will always result in ineffectiveness and in failure to convict the world of the truth of the gospel. Therefore let us examine each element carefully.

(1) *The verbal proclamation.* There can be no question that a verbal worldwide proclamation of the good news of salvation in Christ and of his coming kingdom is foremost in the mission Christ entrusted to his disciples. It was manifest in the training of his disciples; it is evident from the terms used in the Great Commission (preach, teach, evangelize); it was clearly reflected by the primacy given to it by the apostles and early Christians in their daily lives and activities. "He commanded us to preach . . . and to testify . . . ," says Peter (Acts 10:42). "Be it known unto you," Paul cries out as he takes up the mission of Christ, "that through this man [Christ] is *preached* unto you the forgiveness of sins" (Acts 13:38). It is implied in the efforts of the authorities to silence the early Christians, commanding them "not to speak at all nor teach in the name of Jesus" (Acts 4:18; also 5:40, 42). Throughout the book of Acts this is described as being the predominant activity of the Christian church. Nothing could take priority over it.

But what this involves should be made clear. It is not necessarily to be confused with formal sermonizing or to be understood as implying that every Christian must engage continuously in organized evangelistic efforts. It calls rather for ready verbal acknowledgment of the Saviorhood and Lordship of Jesus Christ in all the situations of daily life. It demands ready insistence on the part of the Christian on bringing Christ into every aspect of daily and secular life, even in a society that is oriented in ignorance, indifference, or rejection of Christ and of his claims upon man.

Over and over again, the Christian will find himself in situations — times of human need or moments when the lie is spoken and the ethical principle violated — when he is called upon to declare himself as a witness for his Lord. In such moments silence is not golden; it represents betrayal, and the Lord reminds him of its solemn implications in the words: "Whoever denies me before men, I will also deny before my Father which is in heaven." (But in the midst of such failure in witness, the disciple has also the comfort of Christ's loving dealings with the Apostle Peter in the hour of his denial as a witness.)

In tension with the demand for faithfulness in speaking up for Christ is the disciple's problem of communication — of gaining a hearing and making himself understood. How the Christian reconciles this tension will be the measure of his effectiveness. But the main point to be stressed here is the primacy of the spoken word for every Christian, regardless of his gifts and situation. And we need to be reminded that it was the Holy Spirit who opened the mouths of the disciples and caused them to speak as *he* "gave them utterance."

"O, Lord, open thou my lips, and my mouth shall show forth thy praise," is the petition of one who has been restored to the joy of his salvation and to his calling from the Lord.

This cannot serve as a warrant for any superficial preaching of the gospel, for the use of carnal methods in evangelism, nor for any pharisaical condescension. It is merely to insist that the priority in our Christian mission be placed where Christ demanded that it should be placed. And it is not minimizing its importance to recognize that it must be supported by the other elements of true witness.

(2) *The living demonstration.* The gospel is not merely truth; it is a way and it is a life. Therefore the truth of the gospel must ever become flesh in the concrete situations of

life. The gospel, which is to be announced from the house-
tops, will be sounded out with authority and will command
acceptance only as it is translated into deeds and actions.
This is why Christ made so very clear the distinction between
calling him "Lord" and obeying him as Lord. This is why
love for God is always measured in the Bible by love for man.

Every individual Christian and every Christian community
is, so to speak, a stage upon which the drama of redemption
is played out in the presence of many spectators. And in
the drama of salvation it is essential that the actors be *real*
people, of human flesh and blood, and not "phonies." It is
equally essential that the situations in which they play their
part be also life-situations common to the people around them,
and not hothouse situations of an artificial religious world.

That weakness and defeat play their part in the Christian
life as well as strength and victory must not be concealed.
For the Christian is like an open book, known and read of
all men. It is only in weakness that he is made strong. His
unspoken testimony can be summed up in the words of one
martyr-witness: "I am the foremost of sinners... but I received mercy for this reason, that in me, as the foremost,
Jesus Christ might display his perfect patience for an example
to those who were to believe in him for eternal life" (I Tim.
1:15-16). As men see the struggle with sin and the experience
of divine mercy in the life of such a man, they are enabled
to grasp the love of God for them and understand what
he can do in their own lives. This is part of the Christian
witness.

(3) *The disinterested service.* But this visible portrayal of
the virtues of the gospel and the agony of the Christian
warfare in the life of the Christian and the Christian community must be further supplemented by the demonstration
of power to meet the needs of others. Christians are, so to
speak, the hands and feet of Christ today, who go about
doing good because of his love for men. Hence a third element
in the Christian mission is disinterested service. At the heart
of the gospel preached and demonstrated by Jesus Christ
were concern and compassion for man in every aspect of his

life. He specifically condemned any zeal that is concerned
with selfish ends (Matt. 23:15). He demanded of his disciples
deeds of mercy apart from any ulterior or selfish motives.
"If you salute only your brethren, what more are you doing
than others? Do not even the Gentiles do the same?" (Matt.
5:47).

Consequently it was perfectly logical that the early disciples should pool their resources for distribution to the
poor and needy, and that charity and hospitality should characterize them everywhere. These things were not for purposes
of propaganda; they represented instead a genuine expression
of concern for others. The implications of this for Christian
witness today should be perfectly clear. Only a genuinely
disinterested service to those outside the family, a service
which looks to no recompense, which is not a concealed
means to an end (e.g. the acquisition of more church members), can properly reveal the love of God and the gospel
of free grace. Only such service can deliver the Christian and
the Christian church from the self-interest and ,self-centered-
ness that are at the root of the pharisaism condemned by
Christ.

In the complexity of modern society, it follows then that
social concern and action will form an essential part of the
Christian witness. The church cannot remain indifferent to
the pressing problems that confront men today. In the faithful discharge of his witness, some expression of concern, some
social action must find a place. In faithfulness to the biblical
injunction, and without being diverted from the church's
mission to proclaim the gospel, that concern must be expressed. The important thing is that this imperative be
recognized, and that the door be opened for Christian hearts
to find the means of that outreach in individual, informal,
and collective service to society. This is the badge of true
Christianity.

(4) *The inevitable suffering and death.* It is a paradox
that a witness involving expressions of genuine concern and
true love for others should ultimately culminate in suffering
and death. But this was specifically promised the disciples

by Jesus Christ. In the providence of God, it is part of the witness to be given to the world today.

We recognize that suffering is permitted by God because it is essential to spiritual growth and maturity: we need also to recognize that it is essential as part of the witness to be given the world. "It has been granted to you that for the sake of Christ," says Paul, "you should not only believe in him but also suffer for his sake" (Phil. 1:29-30). Such suffering will result eventually in death. Whether it be death at the hands of enemies (John 21:18-19) or as the result of lifelong service (John 21:21-23) is a matter of indifference. The important thing is to recognize suffering and death as essential elements in the witness that the Christian is called to give.

D. T. Niles has properly placed the finger of truth upon the refusal of the church today to expose itself to danger and suffering. "Jesus was crucified," he says, "because those who rejected Him had the power to crucify Him: the Church in a given situation is too powerful to be crucified."[3] And he rightly reminds us of the truth that "the Lord's death cannot become public in any other way except by the sacrifice and self-denial of those who belong to Him."[4] It is one of the tragic ironies of our modern age that the greatest sacrifice of life in the world's present struggle is being made by non-Christians, and that the Christian should be so comfortable and secure in the midst of it all.

If the Christian church is to make an impact upon the world today, then in faithfulness to God's Word, with disregard of all risks and acceptance of all consequences, it must return to a witness that is characterized by obedience in the verbal proclamation of the gospel, in consistent demonstration of its life, in disinterested service to others, and in the sacrificial spirit that has taken the cross to heart.

---

[3] D. T. Niles, *Upon the Earth,* p. 102.
[4] *Ibid.,* p. 100.

VIII

THE MARTYR-WITNESS IN DAILY LIFE

It is reported that in one of the largest and most evan-gelistic denominations in the United States, 95 percent of the church members have never led a soul to Christ.

Probably one cause for this is the failure of most Christians to experience a sense of specific mission. As laymen in a church framework that relies mainly upon a professional ministry, they do not consider themselves essential to the work of God. Somehow a vision of what each Christian is called to do needs to be imparted. In the following paragraphs we shall seek to provide some practical helps that may help to meet this need.

It goes without saying that the experience of God's saving grace — regardless of the way in which it has been received — is the requisite that qualifies a man to be a witness for Christ. "I believed," says the Psalmist, "therefore have I spoken." A man can only speak of what he knows; he shares only that which he possesses. Paul's testimony expresses perfectly this relation between the experience of grace and the discharge of mission. "For this cause I received mercy," he writes (I Tim. 1:16). But lest there be a tendency to stress experience unduly, and to laud unnecessarily that which is unusual and spectacular, experience must be related properly to several other elements that go to make up witness.

(1) First is the fact of one's humanity. Nothing qualifies a man to speak to other men so much as the fact that he is a man.

Out of the experience of human life with all its elemental struggles and needs, hopes and fears, a man may speak to others. It is as men of like passions — as little, nondescript, mediocre people speaking to others like ourselves (for the world is chiefly populated by ordinary people like ourselves) — that we witness for Christ and bring him into contact with humanity today. Next to the experience of grace, no requisite is so important for witness as the constant recollection of our humanity. This is the point of contact — not Christian experience, not Christian virtues, not dazzling gifts nor personality, but the bond of a common humanity. How much we need to remember this! Herein lies the significance of "a body hast thou prepared me." The potential of mission begins to be perceived with the realization that this body of ours, just as it is in weakness and in strength, in the situation in which God has placed us, is his peculiar instrument for the accomplishment of his will.

(2) Along with appreciation for the basic instrument of contact is recognition of an endowment that is peculiar to each one. It is a common failing to ignore or belittle both the natural and spiritual endowment with which each one is equipped. Hence God is ever calling out to each Christian as he did to Moses, "What is that in thy hand?" in order to open his eyes to the potential with which he has been endowed. In the providence of God that "rod" is a graphic reminder of the necessity of "stirring up the gift of God which is in thee" (II Tim. 1:6).

(3) A further truth to be recognized is that each Christian has been placed by God in a particular situation in which he becomes the key of concrete witness to some specific group.

Therefore an acceptance of one's situation and an awareness of its possibilities form a third element which qualifies the Christian for the witness he is called to give. Like that woman of Samaria who in the moment of her encounter with Jesus suddenly found herself to be the key for the redemption of her entire village, so with each Christian today. Each by virtue of his experience of grace, common humanity, and peculiar gifts, is the key in the particular place in which God has placed him. This is the burden of Paul's argument on the problems of marriage in I Corinthians 7.

The truth of this was brought home forcibly to me recently in the city of Buenos Aires. In the heart of the business district is a famous coffee shop. Among the score or more attendants behind the counter is a simple Argentinian believer who has been used perhaps more than any other Christian to witness to men in high positions in that country. A radiant experience of salvation, coupled with a gift for friendship and a happy knack for pithy communication, combine in this man who stands behind the counter of a coffee shop to make possible a unique and wonderful ministry. Yet every Christian is faced with similar opportunities if he but opens his eyes.

The Christian will not only be conscious of those elements that constitute him a witness but also of the terms of the Commission which sends him forth, and which establishes both the order and the spheres of his witness. Jerusalem, Judea, Samaria, the uttermost part — what is the significance of these words? Perhaps we need to pause over them and meditate upon their meaning for each one of us today. Jerusalem — Samaria — the uttermost part — Is the division only geographic? Do the words merely suggest the ethnic and religious strata of human society? Or do they also remind us that Christ will not allow us to reject (even in our minds) the people who reject and crucify him? He will not allow us to remain behind walls of sectarian, cultural, or racial prejudice. Nor will he allow us to make the gospel the exclusive privilege of one people alone. Therefore, as with the first disciples, his Spirit will be continuously thrusting us out to serve and witness to the very people whom our unconscious prejudice would exclude. We shall find them right at our very door and across the street as well as in the uttermost part of the earth. But our eyes and hearts need to be opened.

In our obedience to the command, it will be helpful to recognize that there are different spheres of witness and that each requires its own method and approach. We have found it of help to distinguish three: (1) the informal witness among the circle of friends and acquaintances with whom our daily life is lived; (2) the witness to be given in the passing and unexpected encounters with strangers along the way; and (3) the organized evangelistic responsibility to which Christ calls every disciple in the fellowship of the church. In each the Christian is responsible, and for each he will need to order his life and activity.

Perhaps the most neglected group is our own friends and neighbors with whom we live in daily contact year after year. Our dealings with them are at best spasmodic and often stilted. We find it easier to substitute a program of organized activity within our church, which takes up our time and energies and effectively cuts us off from those nearest to us. Joseph Bayly has reminded us of this truth in his parable, *The Gospel Blimp*. Begin in Jerusalem, Christ told his disciples; and to the one who wanted the excitement of organized evangelism afield, he said, "Go home to your friends and tell them how much the Lord has done for you, and how he has had mercy on you" (Mark 5:19).

Possibly the reason we neglect those who are closest to us (and this can often include the members of our own family) is the fact that true witness to them requires so much more from us in the giving of time and of ourselves. It involves earning the right to speak, struggling to communicate, and being willing to grapple with the differences and the problems of religious faiths. It is much easier to join with other Christians in the monologue within the church and to sally forth occasionally with them in organized evangelistic expeditions. But Christ would have us start in our own Jerusalem and discover the joy and the rewards of a full, satisfying life of witness that is consciously directed and continuously occupied in engagement and interaction with those around us for the sake of Jesus Christ.

However, in the planning and ordering of such a life, it is necessary also to be alert always to take advantage of the unexpected encounters with strangers whom the Lord brings across our path. The New Testament is full of such encounters — the woman at the well in Samaria, Zacchaeus in Jericho, the lame man on the temple steps, the Ethiopian eunuch, the Roman centurion — and only eternity will reveal the blessings received as a consequence.

Every Christian therefore, without strain and in keeping with his own character and personality, should, in the situation in which God places him, be on the alert for the contacts with strangers that will open the way for the sowing of a seed or for the meeting of a need. He should keep in mind that while he may not intrude uninvited into the sanctum of another man's life, frequently individuals will open their hearts and reveal their needs to strangers, as they will not to friends. He will be aware that the keys that open doors in such encounters are genuine friendliness, sincerity, interest in the other, ease of manner, and willingness to spend time with another person. Without pressing unduly, he will be seeking to make an opportunity to speak of Christ. And he will be alert to ensure a further contact. Some of his greatest experiences in witness will come as a result of the unexpected encounters along the way.

These are some of the factors that qualify and affect the life of the individual Christian as a witness. The important thing is that he should be aware of his opportunity and responsibility. His life and activities should be so planned that the fulfillment of his mission as a witness will occupy the central part. His life in its totality becomes a purposeful witness for Jesus Christ. This is his reason for existence; to this end he was born.

In the discharge of such a witness, he will find it helpful to team up with others. Our Lord sent his disciples out two by two; and the Christian today will receive encouragement, in prayer and planning and perseverance, if he teams up with others, provided it is for the unselfish outreach in home circles and on the job. Team play also furnishes the opportunity for that most essential task of "making disciples" or of being made a disciple in the course of witness to others. Both the younger Christian and the older will contribute to each other's development as together they reach out to others.

As the Christian seeks informally to team up with others in purposeful outreach, he will encounter from the very beginning the existence of walls of separation. In the complex society and constant movement in which people live today, barriers of different kinds have been raised — racial, social, economic, religious. And unfortunately Christians have often erected walls of their own. These must come down. Christ has broken down the walls of partition (Eph. 2:14-16), and the Christian must not build up that which Christ has broken down.

But how can the barriers be broken down? The answer is quite simple. The key to every heart and home is that of unpretentious friendliness. Probably no one can ever estimate the sum total of human woe and misery. There is not a single human being who is not grappling today with problems of loneliness, insecurity, and inner defeat. Everyone stands in need, and the Christian has been placed by Christ in the world to be the neighbor who makes the timely visit.

Therefore a Christian will organize his life — particularly his social life — so as to establish bridges of genuine friendship. Christ has rebuked the tendency to limit one's social life to the Christian friends of his own selection whose company he enjoys or from whose company he profits. "When you give a dinner," he said, "do not invite your friends or your brothers . . . lest they also invite you in return and you be repaid. But when you give a feast, invite the poor, the maimed, the lame, the blind. . ." (Luke 14:12-13). It may take special perception to recognize the needy in these days of affluence, but the Christian must acknowledge in his heart that his social life — as all other aspects of his life — belongs to the Lord. He will also recognize the importance of social visits as frequently enjoined and practiced in the New Testament.

Moreover, the disciple will seek to identify in such ways as he is able with the life and concerns of the community, seeking unostentatiously and disinterestedly to be of service both in personal relationship and civic participation in the life of the community. This will involve acceptance of and struggle with the tensions that are a Christian's inescapable lot in the world — how to remain unspotted from the world and yet identify in love with its need, how to discern between the best and the good in the stewardship of time and money, and other similar tensions. In submission to God's Word and openness to the guidance of his Spirit, he will venture forth, accepting the risks and paying the price, in the knowledge that this is his mission and that the Lord goes with him.

In such a concept of witness, the Christian's home becomes his center of operation for outreach and mission, as do also the homes of his Christian friends, and his own place of business.

Finally, the Christian will always keep in mind the New Testament pattern of training and discipling in the course of evangelistic outreach. As he teams up with other Christians, both young and old, in the work of evangelism, he should be both disciple and teacher — engaged both in the learning process and the teaching process by which the band of disciples may become an expanding, reproductive force. It is thus that the tree grows from the seed, the leaven permeates the mass, and the witness is carried from Jerusalem to Samaria and ultimately to the ends of the earth. Thus will be accomplished the martyr-witness that Christ demands of us all.

IX

THE WITNESSING COMMUNITY

"A TRUE CHURCH," SAYS GEORGE WEBBER, "IS AN OUTPOST OF the Kingdom of God, placed in a particular spot in the world to bear witness to the Lordship of Jesus Christ. A church is a mission living by the foolishness of God in a world that sometimes hates it, sometimes is indifferent, and sometimes seeks to take it captive. Any church that does not recognize the basic purpose for its existence is in jeopardy of its life. The predicament of the church in America is precisely that it does not recognize that it is in a missionary situation."[1]

Alongside such a definition, the average congregation today is revealed as something other than what was originally intended. That may sound shocking. But we are being made to perceive today, by the force of events, by the growing tide of evil and misery around us, and by the criticisms of friend and foe, something of the utter selfishness and self-centeredness of modern church life. Why do we fear to become involved in the tide of human misery and struggle sweeping past our

---

[1] George W. Webber, *God's Colony in Man's World*, p. 29.

doors? Why do we shrink back in the name of dubious harmony and purity from grappling with the difficult problems that beset man in the world of today? What is responsible for our failure in the intercessory prayer, the true holy living, the genuine compassion for the poor and needy that alone can qualify us to proclaim the gospel with authority to the world?

Other criticisms focus on the church's irrelevancy in the secular life of today, its middle-class mentality, its cultic isolationism from the world, its paralyzing divisions, its rigid traditionalism and legalism, and its pious hypocrisy.

Whatever the true situation of the contemporary church as a whole — and we can never forget that the Holy Spirit is continually rebuking his church — it is also well to look on the other side of the picture. There is also a need to see the local church in terms of its strategic position and potential for carrying out God's mission in the world.

So let us look again at the average congregation, and this time let us see it in the light of God's mercy and of Christ's calling. Here is a group of ordinary people, saved by grace and committed to Christ. Their communal life is the arena where the struggle of Christian society takes place, their place of meeting the sanctuary where God is worshiped in spirit and in simple truth.

Let us look at the members of the congregation in their pews and see in them, as A. T. Pierson reminded us years ago, not the passive patients of the pastor but the shock troops for combat,[2] the forces for carrying out the purpose of God, the instruments for witness, service, and missionary outreach in the world today.

Let us perceive, in the light of Scripture's teaching, that every single member, no matter how obscure, has been endowed of God, redeemed and called for service, and that each, in keeping with his experience of grace, endowment and situation, is equipped and ready to be used in the mission of the church. Therefore let us not visualize the congregation

---

[2] A. T. Pierson, *The Divine Enterprise of Missions*, p. 124.

of members merely as the church gathered for worship and fellowship, but let us envision them in their strategic dispersion throughout the community — in the hospitals, dental clinics, schools, business houses, factories, police force, and other centers of activity. It is as they return from the sanctuary to their homes, to their places of business and to the community's centers that they spearhead the witness of Christ.

Let us look again at the pulpit within the sanctuary. It is true that the congregation has become so accustomed to the voice of the pastor that they scarcely listen and that his voice therefore hardly carries to the world outside. But let us not overlook the potential of its teaching and preaching ministry with a captive audience. Here is a time-honored and recognized voice in the community. Imagine the possible impact of a preaching and teaching ministry, week after week, based on God's Word and bearing upon every problem of communal life and witness in such a way as to fulfill God's purpose for it in the world today.

And then finally let us not forget that, in spite of spiritual coldness and inertia and failure in the past, God's Spirit remains among his people — rebuking, correcting, ever recalling to mission, to the redemptive witness for which he brought them into being.

How can a congregation which has unconsciously allowed itself to become cut off from the world around it, and which stands in danger of "losing its candlestick" (Rev. 2:5), awake to new life in mission? Let us advance some suggestions for recapturing the vision, creating the climate, and establishing the pattern of spiritual relevance.

The missionary responsibility of a local congregation must be discharged in ever enlarging circles, "beginning in Jerusalem" and reaching out to the uttermost part of the earth. This is generally accepted by both pastor and congregation, but the important thing is to discover its full implications and possibilities. And these must be perceived not only by the pastor or by a few concerned leaders in the church, but by the entire membership. Only when the entire congregation experiences a sense of mission will it move out in dynamic witness and service. Essential to that experience of mission is a renewed vision — a recognition of its present failure and also of its potential mission, right now and here.

The pastor (who is, after all, the key to the entire situation) cannot communicate this vision merely through preaching and teaching. Part of his responsibility will be the task of gradually involving the members of the congregation so that they begin to see the needs and opportunities around them with their own eyes, and become themselves exercised and concerned in the search for ways to respond. Group studies of the problem may be organized as one step toward imparting a vision of mission. Surveys may be initiated, not with a view to seeking out prospective members for the church but rather to secure an exact picture of the strategic areas of problems and need in the community, as well as to assess the church's capability to contribute toward meeting that need.

Included in such surveys might be an effort to discover and pinpoint the strategic dispersion, vocational as well as geographical, of the membership of the church throughout the community. Any continuous mobilization of forces will require efficient organization, and therefore the building up of a proper directory should be kept in mind also.

Imagination and spiritual comprehension will be needed to discover in the midst of our affluent society what the problems and needs are. Some of them — juvenile and parental delinquency, alcoholism and drug addiction, the modern use of leisure, the loneliness and the lostness of the individual in the mass, sex problems, marital unhappiness and immaturity and divorce — are different from those of yesterday, although the fundamental elements are still the same.

As the congregation begins to hear and see the needs all around it while at the same time it is exposed to biblical obligation in a perspective of relevance, it should begin to experience a growing sense of concern which will stimulate prayer. It is at this stage, and not before, that the prayer life of the congregation on behalf of the need should be promoted. Too often the congregation is urged to pray before eyes have been opened or hearts burdened. The result is the deadly monotone in prayer that kills all initiative and interest. We must not forget that the order demonstrated by our Lord in the training of his disciples was, first, the vision of the multitude's need arousing compassion, secondly, the prayer for laborers, and, finally, the choice and sending forth of the laborers (Matt. 9:26—10:10). This is the logical order.

One minor point to be made here is to suggest that proper use be made of visual and all other media for communicating and keeping before the congregation the results of the surveys and studies that have spelled out the surrounding needs and opportunities. "Make the vision plain," said the Spirit to the prophet of old; and this needs to be done for the entire congregation through every possible medium.

As the vision of opportunity becomes clear and the sense of mission begins to be experienced, it will be necessary for the leaders to think in terms of defining goals and making plans for action. Knowledge that does not result in action spells the end of mission. But action requires leadership, and leadership in congregational witness and service requires much study and planning as well as continuous promotion. It does not come of itself. But in the definition of goals and the formulation of plans it is necessary to keep in mind that the objectives are not to launch artificial, temporary efforts of evangelism, but rather to develop a pattern of church worship, life, fellowship, and service that will be a communal witness in itself and at the same time will provide for and foster the individual witness of its members in the concrete situations of civic life.

To that end it is helpful to remember that the local congregation exists for three purposes: (1) to nourish and support the spontaneous witness of its members who are scattered strategically throughout the community; (2) to furnish that additional and authoritative declaration of the gospel and its implications for all of life which is not possible to the individual members; and (3) to make visible through its communal life, fellowship, and service a foreseeing of the kingdom of God, thus supporting the message preached. The goal of every preparatory effort therefore should be to impart to the entire congregation a vision of the church's responsibility, or its potential ministry in the community, and of the part each member may play in its fulfillment.

Next to recapturing the vision, it is important to create and develop a climate within the congregation that shall not only serve to encourage each member in his daily life of service and witness, but shall also provide the warm atmosphere of welcome and encouragement to outsiders and to new Christians which is essential in any ongoing and successful activity of evangelism. The ineffectiveness of the follow-up of most evangelistic campaigns must be largely attributed to the failure of the local churches in this respect. To correct this situation and to create and maintain the proper climate for witness and service is no easy matter. But the existing climate of indifference, complacency, ingrown exclusiveness, or simple spiritual coldness and deadness must not be tolerated. Whatever the means by which it is achieved, there are certain elements that we believe are essential.

Let us begin, as our Lord began, with *discipleship*. The time has come to give up the unscriptural and ultimately profitless driving for numbers of converts or church members and to return to the fundamental condition Christ laid down for membership in his church. The question may well arise: Did our Lord seek only disciples or did he also have in mind salvation and blessing for the multitudes? This is not the place to answer that question; here we simply reaffirm that for his church Christ sought only disciples, and that to the end of his earthly ministry he did not lay down any lesser condition. His demand is one of absolute commitment for every Christian — this is Christ's goal and God's best for every man.

Such an insistence on discipleship will immediately result in a sifting process, which must be allowed to follow its course. Some will drop away entirely, others will gradually drift to the outer edges of the circle, while a few will move forward into the heart of close fellowship and obedience. But the life and ministry of the fellowship must be carried forward on that basis. No effort should be made to impose an artificial discipline, for the Lord himself is the Husbandman who will do his own pruning. But neither can we relax the conditions that he demanded. The important thing to remember is that the call to membership in the church can be on no condition other than discipleship. And the relationship of pastor to his people must be always that of disciple to disciple in the making of disciples. Every Christian — even the child in the Sunday school — is called to discipleship. Every servant of God must first be a follower of Jesus Christ.

It is in such an atmosphere of discipleship, beginning with the few but always reaching out to press the same demands upon the whole, that the church discovers its mission. Any decision to settle for the discipleship of a select few and to accept a second-class status for the rest is the death of mission. It merely caters to the spiritual pride and ambition of the few and relegates the majority to ineffective passivity.

But how is a disciple made? This is the difficult question. It takes a disciple to make another disciple. It is not a question of mass production or platform lectures. One of the tragic weaknesses of the Christian church today is that too many of its leaders have themselves ceased to be disciples. They have settled instead for fame as experts on evangelism or as missionary statesmen whose pronouncements and exhortations on the subject of Christian mission consequently have little force. It is in the *doing,* in the daily living, the serving and witnessing, that a follower can mature into true discipleship, as disciple begets disciple.

Discipleship begins with an unconditional commitment to Jesus Christ and with the acceptance of a sentence of death. But it takes another disciple to bring that claim home. It is *with* such a man and *from* him, in the *doing,* and not merely the hearing and meditating upon God's will, that the disciple is made. This is a hard saying, and we should not make it harder by laying upon men legalistic and pharisaic burdens that Christ has not called for. But we cannot evade his demands. And it is as the congregation begins to understand, through the example of the committed disciples within its circle, something of the joy and rewards of true discipleship, even in modern circumstances of affluence, that it begins to come into its mission as the body of Christ.

A second element essential to a proper climate of witness is the sense of the presence of God. It is not a matter of aesthetics, of reverence, of order in the service, but a sense of the reality of God in the midst of his people. It cannot be artificially induced, nor prescribed in the church bulletin. It cannot even be accurately defined. But where God is working and the sense of his presence is real, the disciple is encouraged in his witness and the stranger within the congregation is touched and attracted.

Important also as a third element for creating the proper climate of mission is fellowship. In some Christian circles the term is often employed to refer to social life among Christians. Such "fellowship" — too often unconsciously exclusive and self-centered — cuts the nerve of proper witness. It is not Christian fellowship; it contributes nothing to Christian mission and service. One of the greatest needs in Christian circles today is to develop a conscience over such a travesty upon the fellowship instituted by our Lord. It is one of Dietrich Bonhoeffer's contributions to have brought home this truth to many.[3]

The fellowship of Christ is rather a fellowship of disciples who follow their Lord on the road of life, who encounter and share together its problems and burdens, who accept each other regardless of race or position, as sinners saved by grace, who break their bread humbly together at the Lord's table and at each daily meal. It is a fellowship in the world, in service, in witness, and in suffering. Its door is opened to the stranger and the needy, and it is not based on any other distinction but that made by the blood of Christ. It is in the joy and warmth of this sort of fellowship that the seed of the gospel sprouts and grows.

To become a true witnessing community the church must not only capture a vision of congregational mission and create a proper climate. It must also establish the pattern. We say *the* pattern, because what we have in mind is not so much a program of organized evangelistic activities (although they will

---

[3] See, e.g., Bonhoeffer's *Life Together.*

have their place) but the continuous day-to-day life of the church family, which *is* their witness.

Therefore we need to make clear from the outset that we do not refer to the traditional program of church activities, which too often seems to be designed to promote the interests of the church itself. This is not necessarily to imply that the present organizational structures and program of church activities must be done away with. Neither is it to suggest superimposing an added series of organized evangelistic activities to the existing order of regular services. Rather what is suggested is the scriptural ideal and practical possibility of transforming the weekly life and ministry of the local congregation into the dynamic spontaneous outreach of service and witness that Christ intended for it.

Seen from this point of purpose, it becomes evident at once that the entire program of weekly services within the church may need to be revised. A program that hitherto has been geared primarily to serving the members of the church must now be restructured with a view to fitting and stimulating its members for discharging their mission in the community. This need not mean doing away with the old order of service, but it does mean a radical change in its nature and purpose. The Sunday preaching services, the sabbath school, the weekly meetings, the service and social clubs of the church, its ministry of music — these and all the rest of church life may need to be reoriented in line with the proper concept of mission.

Consideration will also be given to the possibility of organizing the congregation into smaller cell groups for more effective training and deployment of each member in the work of Christ. The example laid down by John Wesley and the early Methodists with their "class meetings" should serve to inspire and direct us.

Somehow, without a surrender of the essential biblical distinctives of being a people who live under God's law by grace and are called unto holiness and separation from evil in the world, the church family must refuse to live unto itself, must face outward rather than inward, and must identify itself with the community in its needs and problems and in the light of

God's redemptive purpose. It will therefore always find itself in tension between the command to come out *from* and the command to go *into* the world. Like the early disciples, it will face again and again, in endlessly new situations, the problems of meat offered to idols and of Christian liberty and expediency in the fluctuating demands of relationship to fellow men and to society. But it should experience these tensions and problems in the midst of obedient witness and service.

In line with the distribution of the membership of the local church through all the different sectors of the community, one clearly defined church objective will be to encourage its members in meaningful involvement throughout the community. The keys to open the doors for such a witness are friendship and service — genuine friendship and disinterested service. Avoiding the pitfalls of overly pious and falsely motivated approaches, Christians will be encouraged, through the fellowship and the teaching ministry of their church, to become true friends to those in their neighborhoods and at their places of work and to all those to whom God brings them.

This means that their social life must serve the cause of Christ. And while this may seem a great deal to ask of a Christian, he will discover that his social life is enriched and not impoverished as he surrenders it and uses it for the Lord. And it means that the social life of the church must likewise be surrendered to the cause of Christ — for it is in the life of the church that the pattern will be set for the life of its members.

In addition to showing friendship, the church will seek to follow the example of service laid down by Christ. This service may take countless forms. As in other aspects of its life, the church family will be caught up in the tensions of striking a proper balance in their ministries, but always with God's ultimate purpose in view. Much has been written for and against the church's involvement in social action, civic affairs, and national politics. A minority of Christians tend to polarize at either extreme and would either commit the church officially to the social and political struggles of the day or isolate her completely from them. The majority belong to the inert mass of people that by its passivity and inaction in effect takes a negative stand against all social and political reform.

Somewhere between these extremes there must lie a biblical position wherein the Christian community as a church discharges its responsibility, grappling with the problems and needs but remaining faithful to its calling to proclaim the gospel. The church is not called to solve the problems of a society that has rejected the reign of its Lord. Indeed, it cannot solve them. But it is called in the name and compassion of Christ to serve and to witness to the love of God for mankind. In this area the church functions through its members, who should exert a Christian influence in society on the levels and in the areas in which Providence has placed them.

The church functions also as salt and light by revealing to the world in the life within its circles the harmony of human relationship, social justice, and ethical uprightness which are God's will for all peoples. Therefore the service rendered by the local church in the community will be extended not only individually through its members, but also in that collective contribution to moral and spiritual well-being which as a church it is able to make.

This highlights the need of creative, imaginative approaches for service and witness. For too long the churches have been thinking of service in stereotyped terms of charity and relief for a few individuals at home and abroad, while remaining indifferent to the urgent problems created by the complexities of modern life. Juvenile delinquency, alcoholism, drug addiction, homosexuality, marital unhappiness, and plain loneliness — all represent a challenge to creative Christian thinking. Responses to such challenges will inevitably pave the way for making the gospel clear and for securing for it a sympathetic hearing.

In witness and evangelistic activity, the church may well move beyond stereotyped and traditional approaches in order to show the gospel's relevance to the needy of the neighborhood. With scores of homes available as bases of operation throughout the community, plus the many other media in use today, and with a working force of member disciples, there are no limits to its potential outreach for Christ.

Thus far no hing has been said regarding the official, organized, evangelistic projects sponsored by the church itself. The essential thing for a local church is the dynamic, living witness of its members as a community and in the community. Where this exists the gospel will surely be preached and will commend acceptance, and as a result the church itself will grow. But this is not to do away with official efforts and approaches. Where the membership of the church is functioning in daily discipleship, special efforts will take on greater importance and become more effective means of reaping and following up its daily witness.

During special efforts the church enters fully into its preaching and teaching ministry, thus stimulating its members to further testimony and establishing the new converts in the life of discipleship and witness.

Significantly, the last words of Jesus Christ were directed to local congregations — seven of them — typical of the varieties of congregational life and situation. For each he has a different message according to its need, but the importance of his word to all is the reminder that each exists as a candlestick and that the life and activity of each is to be judged in the light of its faithfulness to its mission. Hence the word of warning: "Remember.... repent and do the works you did at first. If not, I will...remove your lampstand from its place.... He who has an ear to hear, let him hear what the Spirit says to the churches" (Rev. 2:5-7).

Essential to the survival and revival of the local congregations of Christ today is the recovery of the sense of their mission in the world and in the community, and in their obedience to that mission.

X

THE WORLDWIDE WITNESS

We have dealt thus far with the Christian mission on the individual and the local levels. But every Christian and every local congregation seeking conscientiously to discharge its mission is immediately faced with the fact that the Christian obligation goes beyond the local — that it involves worldwide witness. Mission can be taken seriously in the local context only if it is taken seriously in its worldwide extension. It becomes evident upon further reflection that the obligation cannot be worldwide merely in a general sense; if there is any obligation it must be to all nations and to every individual.

In both the Old and New Testaments are revealed God's universal outlook and intent regarding the spread of the gospel. Somehow, in the mystery of God's sovereign working, in keeping with his righteous laws and in spite of the failure of his human instruments, "the earth shall be filled with the knowledge of God," and "unto him every knee shall bow."

Both Old and New Testaments are filled with the truth that God's kingdom will be set up — not as the result of

human accomplishment but ultimately through divine intervention — in power and righteousness. But they are equally
filled with the truth that the labor of Christ's disciples during
this period of waiting for the consummation is not in vain;
rather it represents an essential part of the process by which
God's purpose shall be accomplished and his kingdom established on earth as it is in heaven.

Therefore worldwide mission is imperative. An impelling
force has always called forth the missionary endeavor, sending
the gospel herald on his way to distant lands and to strange
people. It is essential that every disciple, according to his
gifts and calling, and that every local congregation, according
to its resources and situation, participate in the enterprise of
worldwide outreach.

Witness on a worldwide scale, however, has implications
not so clearly apparent on the local level. The encounter with
other religions of equal or greater antiquity, holding the
loyalty of vast multitudes and inextricably woven into the
ethnic and cultural texture of their lives, faces the Christian as
never before with the burden of proving, for himself as well as
for those to whom he goes, the exclusive claims of Christianity.
Implied in the very existence of these other faiths is the challenge: "By what authority?" And it is not enough for the
Christian emissary to assume the rights of free enterprise by
which Coca-Cola or any other American product invades the
foreign market.

The encounter is not only with differing cultures, ideas, and
religions. It is in the area of numbers, of the overwhelming
multitudes which outnumber Christians in the non-Christian
lands by gigantic proportions. The sight of these multitudes,
millions of whom die daily in ignorance of Christ, raises the
big questions regarding the eternal destiny of the so-called
heathen, the mystery of election, and the tempting extra-
biblical notion of an ultimate salvation for all.

The sight of these peoples, creatures of their diverse cultures, also thrusts upon Christian consciousness the vastness
and the complexity of the logistical factors involved in winning a battle to reach a runaway population for Christ. As

the dimension of such a worldwide mission becomes apparent, Christians are made conscious of the imperatives of a united witness and are brought face to face with the full implications of their own divided state. It is no accident that the major impetus given to the modern ecumenical movement toward unity has originated in the missionary and evangelistic frontiers of the world.

The worldwide evangelistic task demands some concrete token of the oneness and unity of the gospel. The Christian senses the necessity of being faithful to basic truths, but at the same time he is aware of traditions that inhibit his full and free response to the demand for unity. The fact that Christians are radically at odds on the question of unity should give pause to any hopes of quick solution. Let those who see cooperation in evangelism as an easy matter seek to understand the importance of the issues involved. Truth is at stake, and truth cannot be compromised. As William Temple has said, "For the Church, commissioned to transmit to all generations the true doctrine which may elicit saving faith, heresy is more deadly than hypocrisy or even than conscious sin."[1]

But let those who would defend the truth remember that truth is more than a theological proposition or a traditional creed. Just as the sabbath was made for man rather than man for the sabbath, so truth must always be related to the living situation. The disciple of Jesus Christ will always live in tension between the demands of righteousness and the demands of love in all his relationships to fellow Christians, as well as to the world. But such tension should not serve as a reason for accepting wrong or unnecessary divisions. It should not provide a basis for refusing to grapple with the problem, nor should it keep us from seeking to correct the situation to the extent that it can be done without compromise or surrender of that which is truly essential.

Obedience to the Great Commission demands unswerving

---

[1] Quoted by Eugene L. Smith, "The Conservative Evangelicals and the World Council of Churches," in *The Ecumenical Review,* Jan., 1963, p. 187.

submission to its terms and faithfulness to its message. We are exhorted in Scripture "to contend for the faith which was once for all delivered to the saints" (Jude 3). We are warned regarding the rise of error and false teaching both within and without Christendom. In the battle between truth and error there can be no surrender nor quarter given to the enemy.

A vital part of the Christian witness, therefore, includes the defense of the truth. And any defense of the truth requires that we guard against the softness that compromises or the legalistic zeal that distorts, the latitude that blurs or the dogmatism that blights. In the struggle to defend the truth it may be necessary to resist the human propensity for confusing one's particular interpretation with the truth itself, to avoid the danger of mistaking nonessentials for essentials, to resist the temptation to make hasty judgments and oversimplified generalizations, and to refrain from using weapons or methods in its defense that are not consistent with the truth itself. But in the defense of the truth there can be no compromise with error.

In the midst of today's war of ideas and doctrines, the chief concern of conservative evangelicals has been to stand true to the faith of the Word of God. Whether interpreting it too narrowly or applying it too zealously, this insistence on the foundations of the Christian faith has been their contribution to the Christian witness in the world today. Though frequently misunderstood and misrepresented, at the heart of their protest is the stand for the reality and authority of the truth as revealed in Christ.

It is an encouragement to conservatives to realize that there are leaders within the historic denominations and in the mainstream of the ecumenical movement who recognize that such a stand for the truth is essential. In an article from which we have already quoted, Dr. Eugene L. Smith of the Methodist Foreign Mission Board[2] speaks as one of the leaders in the National Council, the World Council, and the World Student Christian Federation. Following intimate contact with a

---

2 Now with the World Council of Churches.

group of conservative evangelicals, he was obliged to write as follows: "I began to see them as the true monastics of this age, primarily concerned with the preservation of the faith in its purity in the midst of a collapsing and decadent world — and willing to accept, sometimes without question, the discipline that this requires."[3]

Such recognition is welcome, and it may be that our chief or sole contribution in this day and age is to be a "monastic" one. But every Christian, regardless of his position, is faced with a commission that does not permit him to hide inside sheltering walls but thrusts him out into the world and to its uttermost parts. For the only effective and lasting defense of the truth is to be found in living in daily obedience to its demands.

From the beginning our Lord made clear that obedience to truth was the touchstone of discipleship. Christ committed to his church the task of proclaiming the gospel to "every creature," "among all nations," "to the uttermost part of the earth," and "to the end of the age." Obedience to this command must have top priority. Without in any way deprecating the importance of the doctrinal issues involved, or the essential place other aspects of the church's life must have, it is our conviction that primacy must be given to evangelism. This is her essential reason for existence. This is the most urgent necessity and greatest imperative of the hour.

If evangelism is to have priority, then we must face honestly and realistically all the factors that bear upon the effective and faithful fulfillment of mission. If we take seriously the divine command to preach the gospel to "every creature," then it becomes evident that somewhere, somehow, with due respect for denominational differences and without compromise of doctrinal convictions, some tangible acknowledgment of our joint relationship to Jesus Christ and some convincing testimony to the oneness of the gospel must be given.

For we must recognize that this is not merely a question of the logistics of winning a battle to reach a runaway population

3 Eugene L. Smith, *loc. cit.*

(where only the continuous coordinated witness of all Christians can possibly accomplish the task). It is even more a question of giving consistent and convincing testimony to the truth that there is only one Savior and Lord and one way of salvation. For how can a multiplicity of distinct groups, living and working in isolation or even in competition with each other, testify effectively to a skeptical world that Christ is Lord and Savior?

Is not this the significance of Christ's prayer: "...that they also may be one in us, so that the world may believe..." (John 17:21)? What precisely Christ meant by this and whom he included in his plea for unity needs carefully to be determined. But no wrong definitions of unity should keep the Christian from facing squarely the demand Christ places upon him.

The essential character of this unity is made clear by our Lord's repeated insistence that the disciples love one another, in the knowledge that such fraternal love is a necessary condition for gaining the belief of those who are in the world. But he went beyond that to teach by precept and example that the divine love which culminates in the sacrifice of the cross is to be manifested not only to those within the family but to those without — even to our enemies.

Emphasizing this truth, the writings of the apostles abound with exhortations and instructions regarding the unity of the body and the responsibility of its members. In this simple figure of the body, the founding fathers of the church clearly bring out the truths of its unity, the diversity of its members, and their dependence upon each other.

Today we need to remember that the relationship of member to member is obligatory and not optional (I Cor. 12:15-16, 21). The particular relation, of course, may vary, depending upon the many factors of proximity, maturity, and conduct that govern such ties. One member may comfort, rebuke, or exhort another. If necessary he may even separate another temporarily from active fellowship in disciplinary action — but the basic tie that binds one to another in Christ is never severed. The relationship therefore is not optional. And if this is to mean anything it must be accepted in all the concrete situations of Christian life, fellowship, and service.

Scripture also thrusts upon the Christian the necessity of discernment — of distinguishing between those who belong to Christ and those who do not, and thus of guarding against the ravages of wolves in sheep's clothing. But in making these judgments, let him not go beyond God's Word. Membership in the family of God is not conditioned by full or correct knowledge of doctrine, though such knowledge is by no means to be set aside as unimportant. Certainly membership is not determined by creed, nor form of church government, nor order of service, nor social standing. Therefore let the Christian be slow to exclude any professing Christian from the family of God. And let him remember that if another, no matter what his deficiencies and limitations, does indeed belong to Christ, then they are together part of God's family. And this involves both of them in joint responsibilities for maintaining the unity of the body and proclaiming the gospel of Christ.

The implications of unity in the discharge of mission and in the execution of our evangelistic task are clear enough. Unity (defined always in scriptural terms) is an indispensable requirement; cooperation in evangelism between the members is binding and not voluntary. Because the difficulties of discernment and the problems involved are so many, it is a temptation to draw a hard and fast line based on legalistic propositions and thus settle once and for all the questions of fellowship and cooperation. But this cannot be. Too often such an attitude leads to the evasion of Christian obligation toward one another. It is perilously easy to set up some human standard of orthodoxy and on that basis determine the lines of fellowship and cooperation. But unless one is willing to form the deliberate judgment that another does not belong to Christ, he is not released from his obligation to the other. God does not allow him to say: "I have no need of you." Nor does he allow him to withdraw from the other on the basis that "because I am not the eye, I do not belong to the body."

Even in relationships to those about whom one might have legitimate grounds for doubt, the Scriptures teach a respon-

sibility (Gal. 6:1; Titus 3:10; James 5:19-20; Jude 22, 23).
This does not represent an endorsement of the other person's
views or errors, but it does require that somehow, without
violence to his own convictions and in faithful obedience to
the Word of God as he understands it, each Christian respect
the convictions of the other. And through their common relationship acknowledgment must be made and testimony given
that there is indeed one Lord and one Savior of us all, Jesus
Christ.

A further aspect for consideration has to do with the guidance and working of the Holy Spirit. This too is one of the
cornerstones of the Christian faith, the importance of which
was particularly highlighted by the Reformers in their struggle to recapture the power and purity of the primitive church.

We have already noted the place which the Holy Spirit
occupied in the life and witness of the first disciples. In those
early days of transition in which the church was emerging
from the cocoon of Judaism, the believers were especially
dependent upon the guidance of the Holy Spirit. It was
through his supernatural interventions that their understanding of the Old Testament Scriptures and the oral tradition of
the gospel was enlarged and confirmed.

In the strange developments that resulted in the emergence of a new people of God, they were mindful of the lesson
taught by the example of the leaders of Israel. These Jews
were faithful to the Word of God and zealous for the traditions of their fathers, boasting the greatest orthodoxy. But
they ended up, nevertheless, by rejecting the testimony of the
Spirit and crucifying the Messiah they looked for. What
happened to them could happen again. It can happen today.

Therefore, though faced with seeming contradictions and
the breaking up of cherished institutions and traditions established of old by God, the early Christians acted in obedient
faith. The Apostle Peter summed up this obedience in the
memorable words, "If then God gave the same gift to them
as he did unto us when we believed in the Lord Jesus Christ,
who was I that I could withstand God?" (Acts 11:17).

For today also, we have the Word that says: "Behold, I will

do a new thing" (Isa. 43:19, KJV); "I will work a work in your days which you will not believe, though it be told you..." (Hab. 1:5, KJV); "It shall come to pass in the last days, saith God, I will pour out of my Spirit upon all flesh..." (Acts 2:17, KJV). We do not know precisely the order of final events nor the exact manner of the Spirit's working. We dare not prescribe it and we must be spiritually alert to understand the times. But regardless of our interpretation of scriptural prophecy, the principle is clear and binding: openness to the guidance of the Holy Spirit in the light of the Word of God. We must stand in readiness for the Lord's surprises. "You also must be ready," said the Lord, "for the Son of man is coming at an hour that you do not expect" (Luke 12:40). He may also reveal himself in unexpected ways and places. He is jealous of his sovereignty.

Faced with the divinely given responsibility of proclaiming a universal gospel in the worldwide situation of today, the disciple of Christ, in loyalty to the Truth, must grapple with the problems of an essential unity under the immediate guidance of the Holy Spirit, both in his personal witness and in his communal relationships. Such are the burdens implied by his worldwide task.

XI

EVANGELISM-IN-DEPTH

IN THE PRECEDING CHAPTERS WE HAVE SOUGHT TO PRESENT THE biblical foundation and the normal patterns for Christian life and witness. The responsibility of the individual Christian and that of the local Christian community have been dealt with not only in terms of local fulfillment but also of world-wide outreach. It is hoped that these chapters have convinced the reader that the secret of effective witness and the key to the completion of the Great Commission are to be found not so much in the launching of special evangelistic efforts as in the continuous reproductive life of the Christian "family" as it worships, serves, and witnesses in the course of its everyday life in the secular world where God has placed it. To awaken the church of Christ to this is the goal of "in-depth" evangelism.

Our study of the New Testament patterns, however, has revealed the fact that such a Christian life and witness is best germinated and developed in the climate of evangelistic activity among the multitudes. The task committed is so great, the time allotted so short — if we understand correctly the temper of the New Testament — that every energy must be spent in proclaiming the message of Christ. And the history of the expansion of Christianity confirms the experience of the early Christians that it is as the church gives herself unreservedly to special efforts of evangelism, over sustained periods of time, that she makes an impact upon the world and significant growth takes place.

We come therefore to the organization of special evangelistic efforts on a large scale, confident that the case for mass evangelism and for organized evangelistic witness has been sufficiently established both by biblical example and by the testimony of church history. The immensity of a worldwide task and the urgency of the times call the church to special all-out effort to make Christ known among the nations.

It is in the light of this urgent need that the campaigns of evangelists like Billy Graham and movements such as "Evangelism-in-Depth" (sponsored first by the Latin America Mission) have their place. Such efforts must not be considered as taking the place of the basic indispensable witness of the church in her daily life (without which there can be no fulfillment of the Great Commission). Rather they must be recognized as providing special, repeated opportunities for outreach and reaping. And because the experience gained in efforts of this sort may serve as a pattern for others, they are set forth in some detail.

Born out of the needs and challenges of a missionary situation in Latin America, the movement known as "Evangelism-in-Depth" represents an effort to call the church of Christ back to its principal task and activity. In countries where the community of those who belong to Christ may represent a tiny and weak minority of the population, it sees the need for Christians to join forces and to take the evangelistic offensive. Together they can achieve an outreach that on the one hand is indigenous to the Christian community of the land and not unduly dependent on the activity of special evangelists from outside. On the other hand, it can marshal every available resource, every medium, every Christian agency, and every believer for all-out effort. But such an evangelistic offensive, to be effective and relevant to the needs of the people, must be based on a truly biblical understanding of mission. Hence, the use of the term "in-depth."

Evangelism-in-Depth, therefore, represents both a strategy and a program, a call to action and a way to harness the Christian forces in a given area for the fulfillment of mission. What is involved in such a movement, and the contribution it can make to the cause of Christ in given areas or situations, may perhaps be best perceived by recounting something of how it came into being and was first carried out experimentally in various republics of Central and South America.[1]

The situation in Latin America in recent years has been one of growing opportunity for the gospel arising out of tremendous population increase in the midst of an unprecedented social and technological revolution. Yet at a time of such unequaled opportunity, the validity of the traditional patterns of Christian faith and life was being questioned. As a result, Latin American evangelicals everywhere were becoming increasingly concerned about the task that faced the church of Christ in Latin America and about the proper way to carry it out. Experience in mass evangelism throughout the continent and in the ministry of the local church had strengthened confidence in tried and tested methods of evangelism. But it had also given rise to growing reservations about some aspects of existing church and mission structures and modes of operation.

Foremost was a growing sense of dissatisfaction with the organizational and institutional structure of the foreign missionary society as far as meeting adequately the modern challenge to evangelism was concerned. Foreign missions still had important and strategic functions to fulfill in most fields. But there was an increasing discontent with the projects and programs, which often seemed to represent artificial, top-

---

[1] This account is adapted from the first report of *Evangelism in Depth* published by Moody Press, 1961, and from an article, "Call to Witness," in *The International Review of Missions*, April, 1964. (The story of these early efforts has been further supplemented by a later book, *Revolution in Evangelism*, by W. Dayton Roberts.—Ed.)

heavy, and piecemeal approaches to the job. In tackling the unfinished task, it was instinctive to look to the foreigner, and to modern inventions and techniques which would capture the imagination of the supporting constituency in the homeland because they appeared to promise quick and easy returns. But some years of participation in evangelistic enterprises that were inspired, financed, and executed from abroad had resulted in the conviction that such efforts, while helpful in an auxiliary way, did not represent the true solution. The main task remained almost untouched.

An equal source of concern was the pattern of church life (perhaps a missionary legacy) that was common throughout Latin America. It seemed to represent one major cause for the relative failure of the Protestant churches to witness effectively to the world around them. To see churches facing inward, dedicating more and more of their time and energies to self-centered programs that insulated them from the world, was distressing. Of even greater concern was the growing tendency to depend upon a professional ministry, thus relegating to positions of passive irresponsibility the majority of church members. This pattern of static, self-centered congregational life raised doubts about the future. There could be no real advance for the cause of Christ, no adequate meeting of the present challenge, as long as this trend continued.

A question was also raised by the multiplicity of Protestant bodies and agencies in Latin America and the general picture of division, competition, and confusion that was presented not only to opponents of the gospel, but also to the indifferent public at large and to hosts of well-disposed friends and potential converts. Looked at from a long-range viewpoint, such weaknesses were obstacles to the forward march of the gospel; and the fact that it was not easy to find avenues of fellowship and cooperation in no way banished the problem or lessened the obligation to face it.

Another factor was the resurgence of the Roman Catholic Church in Latin America. Showing new signs of life and vitality, it presented a great challenge to the evangelical movement and raised the necessity of redefining the Protestant stance in relation to Roman Catholicism. Then, too, there was the continued rapid increase and spread of the sects, creating problems of relationship and adding to the general religious confusion and disorientation. There was also the relentless permeation of Marxist and socialist ideas into a soil made fertile by economic pressures and political instability. And looming over all was the spectacle of a continent caught in the throes of an unparalleled population explosion. All this called for a careful reevaluation of present evangelistic programs and practices, and for a fresh consecration to the task. Could the challenge be met? If so, how? What was the secret of successful expansion? The search for the answers to these questions led in different directions.

One consequence was to carry out a study of the factors responsible for rapid expansion or relative stagnation in the experience of various movements in Latin America. Eventually such studies led to the drawing up of a tentative conclusion, which was worded as follows: *The expansion of any movement is in direct proportion to its success in mobilizing its total membership in continuous propagation of its beliefs.* This alone is the key.

Once this conclusion was phrased, it was no great surprise to discover that it led directly back to the norms and practices of the first-century church. But further reflection suggested the additional truth that for an expanding movement to retain its essentially Christian character, it must carry out its witness in conscious submission to the Word of God, and to the energizing and directing operation of the Holy Spirit. Apart from this, any movement, no matter what its outward accomplishments or success, will ultimately depart from course. All the same, the key to successful expansion is the continuous witness of the totality of the disciples.

If this is true, how can it be done? The effort to elaborate some sort of practical program for implementing the key principle of expansion defined above led first of all to setting down certain premises or objectives that, it was believed, should be incorporated in the plan. These were as follows:

(1) Every Christian without exception is called upon to be a witness for Christ. The momentum of a church carrying out its witness is directly affected by the degree to which its members participate. Therefore the mobilization of the total membership must be the goal, even though the ultimate result may fall short of absolute attainment. In the case of the older and less dynamic communities, it may be necessary to depend finally upon an inner core of active disciples; but the idea that passive membership in the church of Christ is a legitimate option should be strongly discouraged. Each Christian should be encouraged to discover and develop the mission for which he is fitted. And to carry out this process is one of the primary responsibilities of the leaders of the church.

(2) Personal witness must center in the life and fellowship of the local congregation. This involves recognition of the true mission of the local church as a testifying community, set down in the world not for purposes of self-seeking or self-defense but for disinterested service and faithful witness in a climate of spiritual worship and genuine brotherhood.

Probably the greatest contribution of any national movement of Evangelism-in-Depth is the vision it can impart to local congregations regarding the true mission of the local church. Wrong patterns and habits of self-centered activity can be broken and new patterns of dynamic service and witness started. In the final analysis, the success of such a movement will be measured by the new life imparted to the local congregation. And obviously, this most important of goals is also the most difficult to attain.

(3) The witness of the individual Christian and the local congregation must relate correctly to the total witness of the universal church. The mechanics of giving concrete expression to the unity of the body of Christ involves no end of problems and brings up delicate questions of relationship — both individual and organizational. These cannot be minimized and should not be evaded. Involved, furthermore, is the necessity of clear and scriptural definitions of unity and fellowship, along with common-sense and practical approaches to problems of cooperation in evangelism. Nor can the teach-

ing responsibility that pertains to the preaching of the gospel be overlooked. But it is imperative that the responsibility of unity and fellowship in witness be faced.

Too often, it seems, evangelical groups shy away from the question of responsible relationship to other Christian groups. One of the amazing features of American Protestantism on the local level is the multiplicity of local congregations existing year after year, side by side, in almost complete ignorance and indifference to each other. Each group tags the others as deficient or divergent in doctrine or practice (as if that settled the matter), and on this basis lines of communion and activity are drawn and a wholly separate existence pursued. The differences in doctrine or practice, the organizational problems of cooperation, and an undue sense of responsibility for the denominational distinctives are advanced as sufficient reasons for refusing to relate to the other groups.

Certainly absolute loyalty to the truth is essential — even to the point where a tragic choice that ruptures unity may have to be made. But every evangelical will still have to face the demands of his relationship to all the other members of the body, in the indispensable part that this relationship must play in the testimony given to the world by the church of Christ.

Any thorough grappling with the universal terms of the Commission — any serious effort to discharge mission — inevitably forces the evangelical conservative to face the imperative of giving tangible witness to the oneness of the body of Christ. This is obligatory and not optional. And one of the glaring blind spots in many Christian circles is the ignorance of or indifference to this great body of biblical truth.

(4) The witness of all individuals and communities must aim at nothing less than total and complete outreach. The mandate specifies "every creature," "among all nations," "in all the world." Only a literal acceptance of these terms can command the active enlistment of every Christian. Therefore the activity planned for the Christian forces must include the specific objective of reaching the entire area.

That the task is constantly renewing itself with every new generation in no way diminishes the responsibility for aiming at total outreach. On the contrary, it accentuates it. But at the same time, it offers no justification for thinking in terms of noisy, superficial activity that is little more than ill-conceived proselytism. One rightly draws back from the ambitious programs of evangelistic conquest that give all too much evidence of being conceived in the energy of the flesh. Such efforts tend to be artificial and superficial, and to drain off the energies that are needed for the fulfillment of the daily tasks of service and involvement in the world. There is always the danger, also, that they may become ends in themselves.

But the Christian is never allowed by the Spirit of God to forget that God loves the whole world, that "he is not willing that any should perish," that his Son died for all, that all might hear. The command weighs upon every disciple on behalf of every creature. Universality and uniqueness — fundamentals of the gospel we preach — are truths that can only be established by obedient action. And to the extent that the profound sense of these truths is lost, to that extent the church enters into the hypocrisy of professing what it does not really believe or practice, and the nerve of evangelism and mission is cut.

Therefore, without fanaticism, but in adherence to scriptural norms and methods, and in true dependence upon God's Spirit, the call must sound out: *total mobilization for total evangelization.*

With these premises or goals in mind, a plan of action has been drawn up. It involves first the idea of bringing together the entire Christian leadership of a given area for a retreat in which, as they wait on the Lord, primary consideration can be given to the evangelistic task that needs to be carried out. This logically inaugurates a preparatory stage of mobilization, in which every effort is made to publicize the program, organize the necessary committees, and get the movement under way.

Most important is the formation of hundreds of small

prayer cells — units of three or more persons meeting regu-
larly in homes and other places — to pray for the evangelization of their country. Each of these cells will subsequently
serve as a nucleus for Bible study, for informal witness and
visitation, and for active participation in the organized evangelistic efforts to be carried out.

A second stage, to follow immediately, involves an inten-
sive training program, organized according to local conditions on denominational or interdenominational lines, and
aimed at enlisting and training hundreds of Christians for
active service in the daily witness of their church and in
the united effort of nationwide evangelism. During this stage
it is expected that a special ministry of teaching will be carried out among the local churches with a view of imparting
to pastors and their congregations a new vision of their potential service and witness in the community.

A series of formal evangelistic efforts, organized and carried out according to the demands and opportunities of the
local situation, is the next phase of the program. House-to-
house visitation, open-air evangelism, literature distribution,
special approaches to special groups, local church conferences,
and united evangelistic crusades should all be combined for
the purpose of mobilizing the greatest number of Christians,
making the strongest possible impact upon the entire area,
and embarking upon a practice of continuous outreach and
activity.

These efforts, carried out over a period of months, require
careful follow-up. Converts need instructions, new prospects
should be visited, newly organized congregations need to be
consolidated, and unreached areas need to be entered. Of
equal importance is the need to consolidate the gains made
in fellowship and cooperation between the different groups.
And hundreds of Christians who have been drawn into active
witness and service need encouragement and further training.
In the final analysis, the success of the entire movement must
be measured, not by attendance figures or numbers of decision cards signed, but by the continuing dynamic witness
of Christians and their congregations.

Experiments with such a program on a national scale have taken place in various republics of Central and South America and have been very encouraging. Reports of these experiments have awakened a widespread interest that was completely unexpected. It was not so great a surprise to receive letters of inquiry from other Latin American republics, but considerable correspondence has come from other parts of the world as well, with the question: Is Evangelism-in-Depth practical for our country too?

Special encouragement has come also from Christian leaders in different places. Describing Evangelism-in-Depth as a new dimension in evangelism, Arthur Glasser, Home Director for North America of the Overseas Missionary Fellowship, wrote as follows:

> What could be more dead-center to all the debate about missionary strategy? Not the Western missionary going on his own, but the Western missionary identified with the national church as it moves out in all directions.... In present missionary thinking, I see nothing comparable with its vision and dynamic.... This marks a heartening break-through in the sinful tangle of inertia that has delayed for so long the advance of the Gospel both at home and overseas.[2]

Whether the program of Evangelism-in-Depth developed in Latin America is adaptable to every part of the world remains to be seen. Perhaps this report will encourage further experiments.[3] It should serve at least to focus on two simple propositions that ask today for conscientious and prayerful consideration. These are:

First, that the Great Commission with its universal goals must be taken seriously, and that the primary Christian task in the world today is the faithful and obedient discharge of that responsibility.

Second, that the key to the successful fulfillment of the Great Commission lies in the mobilization of every Christian,

---

[2] From a review of *Evangelism in Depth,* published in the *Evangelist,* November-December, 1961.

[3] Since this was written, Evangelism-in-Depth principles have been successfully applied in Nigeria, Congo, the United States and elsewhere.

for the expansion of any movement is in direct proportion to its success in mobilizing its membership for continuous propagation of its beliefs.

Evangelism-in-Depth therefore is not only a simple plan of action for mobilizing Christian forces in evangelistic outreach. It also represents a call to action now.

"The Holy Ghost saith today."

XII

"FOR THIS CAUSE, I . . ."

THROUGHOUT OUR STUDY WE HAVE SOUGHT TO SHARPEN OUR understanding of the mission that has been committed to the Christian and to the Christian church in the world. To that end, we have focused briefly on the principal problems and challenges being faced today. Modern scientific secularists' rejection of the basic presuppositions of supernatural Christianity, the challenge of other religions and religious sects, the massive onslaught of materialistic communism, have all formed part of the picture. The theological tensions within Christendom that originated in the reaction of existentialism against traditionalism, and particularly against the conservative evangelical tradition, have been seen as factors affecting not only the church's definition of its mission but also of the goals, strategy, methods, and programs employed for the realization of that mission.

In the light of these challenges, and always with the mounting needs of a multiplying world in revolutionary transition before us, we have sought to rediscover the principles and patterns for the discharge of mission that are laid down in Scripture, and to suggest some practical applications for the life and witness of the ordinary Christian and of the average Christian congregation in the environment of today's world.

We come now to the end of this study, conscious of its limitations but grateful for the opportunity afforded by Fuller Seminary to lecture on such a subject.

During these past months the exciting story of the beginnings of the witness of the Christian church as told in the book of Acts has been constantly before us. Its normative character for our life and witness has been deeply impressed upon us. Over and over again — such is the indivisible unity of Christian experience and of sacred history — we have noted the similarities between the first century and ours. In the light of the approaching consummation of this age, the closing scene of the book of Acts seems to sum up, in the beauty of biblical symbolism, both the predicament and the opportunity that characterize our Christian situation in the turbulent world of today and that define our reason for being — our God-given task and responsibility.

Descriptions of man's struggle for survival in the storms of the seas have always been among the most fascinating of all literary accounts of human experience. They form an impressive part of the biblical story. Something of the rise and fall of human hope and anguish is captured by the Psalmist in the words:

> They that go down to the sea in ships, that do business in great waters;
> These see the works of the Lord, and his wonders in the deep.
> For he commandeth, and raiseth the stormy wind, which lifteth up the waves thereof.
> They mount up to the heaven, they go down again to the depths: their soul is melted because of trouble.
> They reel to and fro, and are at their wit's end.
> Then they cry unto the Lord in their trouble, and he bringeth them out of their distresses.
> He maketh the storm a calm, so that the waves thereof are still.

Then are they glad because they be quiet; so he bringeth them unto their desired haven (Ps. 107:23-30, KJV).

No one who has read Luke's vivid description of the storm that overtook Paul and his companions as they were being transported to Rome can have failed to recall the strange story of Jonah, caught centuries before in an equinoctial gale in the same sea. And somehow in the reading of each account one senses a symbolic significance that reaches far beyond the historic incidents themselves.

No biblical description of a storm at sea is so vivid, and, according to the judgment of modern sailors, so accurate as Luke's account. The details of shipping in those days, the record of weather and change, the descriptions of the Roman soldiers and of the ship's crew, are all true to life. In that Alexandrine bark, lurching through the darkness of the storm and swept by the waves of the gale, and in that band of 276 souls desperately struggling to survive, we see symbolized the whole of humanity, all in one common peril of destruction. Merchants, soldiers, sailors, and passengers — all are prisoners of the boat and of the storm, and all are at their wits' end.

But attention is focused by Luke upon one man in the midst of the storm. There he stands on the heaving deck of the ship while all around him sound the awesome crashing of wind and waves and the desperate cries of human beings. Everyone else but he is busy lightening the ship, tightening the stays, seeking desperately to preserve the life of the ship. There he stands. But what good is he? Of what use in the emergency of an hour that calls for action?

What good is the Christian in the world today? Of what use is he in the world's present upheavals? What has he to offer in a day that calls for action — scientific know-how, technical skill, and collective endeavor? He seems almost to be irrelevant, worthless — an idle passenger in a ship where every hand is needed for survival.

It is in this moment of darkness and despair that Paul steps forth to call out the words of hope and good cheer that give assurance of salvation and lend purpose to human effort, buoying up the fainting spirits of those on board. As the hurricane spends its violence and drives the ship before it, it is the Christian apostle who furnishes the hope, the inner strength, and the practical wisdom that eventually bring every man safe to shore, even as the ship is pounded to pieces by the waves. So in the end it turns out that it was not so much the navigating skill of the ship's captain, nor the centurion's enforcement of order, nor the frenzied efforts of crew, soldiers, and passengers (though each had its place), but the supernatural intervention of God in answer to one man's prayer.

The turning point in the storm as described by Luke is that moment when Paul first steps forth to speak the words of hope. "Take heart," he cries, "for there shall be no loss of life among you, but only of the ship." What brings to Paul the assurance of deliverance is revealed to be his encounter with the angel of God in the midst of the storm. It is the word of God given to him in the night of the storm that constitutes the grounds of his certainty. "Do not be afraid, Paul," the angel had said, "you must stand before Caesar; and lo, God has granted you all those who sail with you." So he cries, "Take heart, men, for I have faith in God that it will be exactly as I have been told."

Probably no words can describe the impact made upon a fearful and fainting heart by the resolute note of confidence and cheer struck by one who has met the Lord. It is in this emergency that the prisoner of Christ justifies his existence and fulfills the purpose for which he has been placed in the ship. In so doing he becomes the living example of what every Christian is called to be in his own world and time.

As one reflects upon Paul's bearing in the storm, one is impressed with the reality of his concern for all those on board. It was not a question of his own personal security. That had been promised even before he boarded the ship (Acts 23:11). Nor was it a question of the salvation of his personal companions. Love knows no limitations, makes no distinctions, sets no bounds to its claims. "God has granted you *all* those that sail with you." What a remarkable disclosure of the prayer burden of the apostle in that hour of peril! Selfish owners, who were willing to imperil the lives of those on board for the sake of material gain, brutal soldiers with their cynical contempt for human life, ungodly sailors interested only in their own deliverance — with all of them Paul was identified, and for all of them he prayed.

Paul's example stands as a rebuke to our own self-centeredness today. It stands in contrast to our tendency to withdraw from the world's agony, to save ourselves, to stand prudishly aloof, indifferent to the fate of the unreligious men and women with whom, nevertheless, we sail in the storm of life.

Paul's genuine concern found its expression in different ways. First in the intercession that resisted all instincts of self-preservation, and against all natural appearances' and possibilities pled for the lives of all those on board. Like a Moses standing between the judgment of God and God's people, so was Paul in the night of the storm.

Not only in intercession is this loving concern expressed, but also in the practical actions he took to communicate the word of hope, to minister to the bodily needs of those on board, to guard against the malice of men, to guide to safety on shore and there to kindle the fires of human warmth and fellowship. True intercession is always accompanied by practical service, and this too is an essential part of the function of the Christian on behalf of those who voyage with him in the ship of life.

The situation in which the world finds itself today has been described by many of the world's leaders as the greatest crisis of all history — a storm in which civilization seems doomed to go down. By the grace of God, there is aboard ship a handful of Christians who can, by virtue of the word that God has given, be instruments of hope and salvation for those on board.

It is for this that they exist. And this is the hour of their destiny.

BIBLIOGRAPHY

Some titles that have been helpful in the study of Mission and Evangelism

Allan, Tom. *The Face of My Parish.* New York: Harper, 1953.

Allen, Roland. *Missionary Methods: St. Paul's or Ours?* London: World Dominion, 1956; Grand Rapids, Eerdmans, 1962.

———. *The Spontaneous Expansion of the Church and the Causes Which Hinder It.* London: World Dominion, 1927; Grand Rapids: Eerdmans, 1962.

Anderson, Gerald H., ed. *The Theology of the Christian Mission.* New York: McGraw-Hill, 1961.

Barth, Markus. *The Broken Wall.* Valley Forge, Pa.: Judson, 1959.

Bayly, Joseph. *The Gospel Blimp.* Havertown, Pa.: Windward, 1960.

Blauw, Johannes. *The Missionary Nature of the Church.* New York: McGraw-Hill, 1962.

Boer, Harry R. *Pentecost and Missions.* Grand Rapids: Eerdmans, 1961.

———. *That My House May Be Filled.* Grand Rapids: Eerdmans, 1957.

Bonhoeffer, Dietrich. *Ethics.* New York: Macmillan, 1961.

———. *Life Together.* New York: Harper, 1954.

de Dietrich, Suzanne. *The Witnessing Community.* Philadelphia: Westminster, 1958.

Ferm, Robert O. *Cooperative Evangelism.* Grand Rapids: Zondervan, 1958.

Hamel, Johannes. *A Christian in East Germany.* New York: Association, 1960.

Hoffer, Eric. *The True Believer.* New York: Harper, 1951.

Johnson, Robert Clyde, ed. *The Church and Its Changing Ministry.* Philadelphia: The United Presbyterian Church in the USA, 1961.

Kraemer, Hendrik. *The Communication of the Christian Faith.* Philadelphia: Westminster, 1956.

121

————. *A Theology of the Laity*. Philadelphia: Westminster, 1958.

Latin America Mission. *Evangelism in Depth*. Chicago: Moody, 1961.

Latourette, Kenneth Scott. *A History of the Expansion of Christianity*. N.Y.: Harper, 1937-1945.

Lindsell, Harold. *A Christian Philosophy of Missions*. Wheaton, Ill.: Van Kampen, 1949.

McGavran, Donald A. *The Bridges of God*. London: World Dominion, 1955.

————. *How Churches Grow: The New Frontiers of Mission*. London: World Dominion, 1959.

Mooneyham, W. Stanley, ed. *The Dynamics of Christian Unity*. Grand Rapids: Zondervan, 1963.

Nee, Watchman. *The Normal Christian Church Life*. Washington, D.C.: International Students Press, 1962.

Neill, Stephen. *Creative Tensions*. London: Edinburgh House Press, 1959.

————. *The Unfinished Task*. London: Lutterworth, 1957.

Newbigin, J. E. Lesslie. *A Faith For This One World?* New York: Harper, 1961.

————. *The Household of God*. New York: Friendship, 1954.

————. *One Body, One Gospel, One World*. London: Edinburgh House Press, 1958.

Niles, D. T. *That They May Have Life*. New York: Harper, 1951.

————. *Upon the Earth*. New York: McGraw-Hill, 1962.

O'Connor, Elizabeth. *Call to Commitment*. New York: Harper, 1963.

Packer, J. I. *Evangelism and the Sovereignty of God*. Chicago: Inter-Varsity, 1961.

Pierson, Arthur T. *The Divine Enterprise of Missions*. A condensation; Colportage Series. Chicago: Moody, 1898.

Raines, Robert A. *New Life in the Church*. New York: Harper, 1961.

Rinker, Rosalind. *You Can Witness with Confidence*. Grand Rapids: Zondervan, 1962.

Roberts, W. Dayton. *Revolution in Evangelism*. Chicago: Moody, 1967.

Robinson, John A. T. *Honest to God*. Philadelphia: Westminster, 1963.

Smith, J. Edgar. *Friendship Evangelism*. Anderson, Ind.: Warner, 1959.

Webber, George W. *God's Colony in Man's World*. New York: Abingdon, 1960.

INDEXES

I. Subjects

II. Authors

III. Scripture